Antigua

by

Rachel Q. Smith

To Jean

Remember life starts the minute
you step out of your
Comfort Zone!

Rachel x

Spire
Publishing
www.spirepublishing.com

Spire Publishing - December 2011

First published in Canada and the UK 2011
by Spire Publishing Ltd.

Chart image reproduced with the permission of the UK
Hydrographic Office, the Canadian Hydrographic Service and
the National Geospatial-Intelligence Agency.

Eminem lyrics are property and
copyright of their owners.

A cataloguing record for this book is available from the Library and
Archives Canada. Visit www.collectionscanada.ca/amicus/index-e.html

Designed by Spire Publishing Ltd.
Salt Spring Island, BC, Canada

www.spirepublishing.com

Printed and bound in the USA or the UK
by Lightning Source Ltd.

ISBN: 978-1-926635-63-7

Armed with 3 pairs of oars, 3,500 baby wipes, enough food to sink a battleship, a sense of humour and a 'can do' attitude, this is the story of how two determined women changed from non-rowers to Atlantic rowers, raising thousands of pounds to help those affected by breast cancer in the process.

Foreward by Dee Caffari

Camping can be fun and exciting. Rowing a boat on a lake can be relaxing and entertaining. Combining the two for months on end across an ocean is scary, at times terrifying and an opportunity of a lifetime. Rachel and Lin took on this challenge.

The rollercoaster of emotions felt during an adventure as exhilarating as rowing cross the Atlantic Ocean is extreme. The good times are really good and memories remain etched in your subconscious forever. The bad times can be really bad, but we have this amazing ability to pack these bad experiences into suitcases and lock them up in a dark recess of our minds. We learn from these experiences but we do not dwell on them. We turn negatives into positives and find a hidden strength to overcome the setbacks and push on. After all we have people following our adventure, investors wanting to see great results and an objective we have set that we want to fulfil. These are the characteristics of adventurers that push boundaries, live outside their comfort zones and challenging what is normally accepted.

Rachel and Lin, by taking on and completing the row across the Atlantic Ocean, have joined a very elite few to have been successful at such an extreme activity. They are inspirational women and high achievers. With a background in dragon boat racing at a world class level, tough competition was nothing new. As a world class athlete, Rachel was aware that being physically at her best was not enough. A large amount of success comes down to being psychologically prepared too. This knowledge contributed to the success but was probably underestimated in its importance during the build up to the race event. When you read this detailed and honest emotional account of how Rachel got to be there and what it was really like, you travel through the same emotions. You feel the same anxiety and then glow in the glory when struggle, fear and bloody hard work are all worth it as you cross the finish line.

As my message to them before the start said, 'you can do more than you think you can, you just have to dare to dream.'

Dee Caffari MBE
First woman to sail solo, both ways around the world.

Introduction

Rowing an ocean is not for everyone, and of those who attempt to take it on, few get to the start line and even fewer make it all the way across. It's pretty similar to life in general I think, with all its ups and downs! But if you don't at least try, you'll never know whether you can do it. For Lin and I, it was a bit like the phrase 'if you say you can, or you say you can't; you're probably right.' Well, we thought we could, so we set out to prove it – to ourselves and everyone else!

From the moment when Lin and I first started to discuss rowing across an ocean it really was a challenge that we believed we could complete. There are other challenges we considered, but we both felt a special attraction to this particular one for some reason. It turned out to be both the best and the worst thing we'd ever done... but we survived to tell the tale.

But this story is about so much more than two crazy women who decided to take on the challenge of rowing across the Atlantic. It's about the team of people who supported and encouraged us every step (or stroke!) of the way, those who believed in us even when our own belief wavered and the generosity of those who paid out their hard earned cash to help us on our way. It's about the people who sent such amazing messages while we were at sea, the inspiration we took from those we met, and the lasting friendships we made on our amazing journey. It's also about everyone affected by breast cancer in some way, and the £65,000 raised by this campaign to help Breast Cancer Care to support them.

To each and every person who contributed to this challenge in some way; any way, we send our heartfelt thanks to you. We quite simply couldn't have done this without you.

Enjoy the story!

Chapter 1

'Watch out! I could see the wave building some way behind us and yelled the warning to Lin, literally just in time. Lin followed my gaze as my eyes rose up to meet the rapidly changing horizon. No questions asked she jumped up from the deck where she was preparing lunch and whipped around, lightening fast, to slam shut the main hatch into our cabin. Although she couldn't see what was behind us, she knew from my expression that this was serious. It had been a rough day so far anyway, the huge waves tipped with angry, foaming white crests hummed and gurgled around the hull of our boat in quick succession. But instinct told me that this one meant business.

All we could do then was wait and that few short seconds seemed like a life time as the wave grew, curling up and around, bright blue and beautiful, yet menacing and deadly, to meet us broadside. It crashed right over the top of Barbara Ivy, our little pink rowing boat with incredible force. I dived from the rowing seat towards the wall of water, in an automatic yet vain attempt to stabilize the boat, while Lin was hanging on for dear life to the oars that were strapped diagonally down each side of the boat, waiting for the inevitable and telling herself to 'hold on, just hold on'.

It was far worse than anything we'd experienced before as we were submerged in a foaming, bubbling mass, our little boat skidding sideways at an impossible angle, completely swallowed up by the water. We couldn't see each other by then, we were lost in our private dread, knowing that our worst nightmare was playing out right there and then. It was as if we had become part of the ocean itself and the next thing I remember was the sound of it all around, swooshing and gurgling. I wrenched my left foot painfully out of the steering shoe and opened my eyes to see bright blue all around, surprisingly clear and beautiful. I knew I was under the water, but had no idea of which way was up until silvery bubbles heading towards the surface gave me a lead and I kicked out gratefully to follow them to the open air.

I popped up right next to Lin, with a gasp of air we looked at each other in complete and utter disbelief.

'Are you OK?' she asked shakily, wiping her wet hair out of her eyes,

'Yup, you OK?' I replied, stunned, heart pounding and not quite sure what had actually happened. We looked around to take stock. We were both still wearing our harnesses and clipped on to the boat, which was the right way up but listing heavily to one side above us, filled up to the gunwales and with water gushing out of her scuppers. We were still being carried over the peaks of the massive waves at some speed, although they seemed maybe just a little less vicious and violent than before; now they'd done their damage.

It did take us a few seconds to work out what had actually happened and how we came to be bobbing around in 5,000 metres of Atlantic Ocean. We didn't quite believe that we could have capsized at first; it just didn't seem possible to us and we'd had such faith in the boat. But the realisation soon hit that we really had survived the boat rolling 360 degrees, and it actually reduced us to helpless giggles as we watched a water bottle and compass disappearing over the top of a wave. Next, Lin's lunch (dehydrated cod and potato) floated past she reached out to grab it, throwing it unceremoniously back up into the boat with the comment "I'll be having that later!" By this stage of our adventure, cod and potato was a real treat and it seemed Neptune would have to do more than capsize us in order to part Lin from her lunch!

We both carried out a quick check of heads, arms and legs for any obvious damage. Luckily we found that all limbs were fully attached and in reasonable working order, while we were relieved to see the water around us was clear and blue, indicating that there were no obvious cuts or bleeding. We sincerely hoped we wouldn't have to worry about attracting unwanted attention from the local shark population!

While we still didn't fully appreciate our pretty dire predicament at that precise moment, it was apparent that our immediate options were limited. We knew we were 300 miles from the nearest land as we'd been planning to quaff our celebratory '300 miles to go' mini bottle of Champers with our lunch. But it looked like priorities needed to change quickly and Champagne was definitely not top of the list.

There is no one around to help in the middle of the ocean. You're on your own and therefore you have to deal with whatever it throws at you. We knew there were no nearby ships, helicopters can't fly that far and our support yachts were miles away. But all of that went unmentioned as we decided that the first step was to get back in the boat and assess the situation, before looking at the best options and coming up with an action plan.

Lin was a bit tangled up in the bungees used to fix our water tanks in place on deck, so I volunteered to clamber back onboard first. With one foot hooked in the grab ropes running down the side of the boat, I hauled myself over the gunwale, flopping and slithering onto the deck a rather undignified manner and doing a good impression of a big wet fish in the process.

A scene of carnage faced me as I slowly got my balance and stood up. Making my way gingerly down the wet deck of the boat, I leaned over to disentangle Lin and gave her a hand up onto the deck. We gave each other a hug as we gazed around in wonder at the equipment strewn across the deck, while a snapped oar flapped around dangerously in the rough conditions. Massive waves continued to thunder by, their white tops fizzing along Barbara Ivy's hull as the wind whipped our dripping hair round our faces. But in contrast, the sun was warm on our skin and we knew we wouldn't chill, even in our shocked state.

Still stunned we both seemed to go straight into autopilot mode and started to bail water out of the main foot well. Bit by bit we cleared up the debris and stowed away the bags that had shifted. We made a list of the things we'd lost to Neptune and as we worked we found that everything important was still lashed down and the only items missing were the drinks bottle, Lin's left hand glove, my sunglasses, a compass and probably most important of all - the lid from the toilet bucket seat! We were amazed as we realised that we had spares of all these items.

As I changed the broken oar for a new one, joking about keeping the broken halves as a souvenir, Lin noticed that even more bizarrely, the cooking equipment which hadn't been fastened down, and for which we had no spares, was all still there. The kettle and cooker were both on deck, wedged under opposite gunwales by some centrifugal force created as the boat rolled. Our matches were lying on deck, still dry in their plastic bag - the now soggy rubbish bag was still onboard and our spoons tucked loosely underneath the ropes holding down the life raft. Incredible!

Although we hadn't felt any pain at first, as the adrenaline started to subside we noticed some swellings and colourful new bruises forming on our limbs. I had a nasty one on my left arm and

11

as I ran through the possible culprits, I realised that the most likely cause was the steel frame of the rowing seat that I'd been sitting on when we went over. I shivered a little as I realised that when it fell off the rowing rails and was spinning around in the water attached by its lanyard, those sharp, solid metal corners would have been somewhere near my head. It wasn't a pleasant thought.

Although we tried not to focus on it too much right then, and we certainly didn't voice it out loud, the thought was starting to sink in that we were lucky to have escaped with our lives. There were no broken bones, no cuts, no real pain - our boat had self-righted exactly as she was designed to, and the most important loss to the ocean was the loo lid! If there is such a thing as guardian angels, then we definitely had ours with us that day, probably working overtime. I wondered how many of our nine lives we had left!

Still a little disorientated, we decided to continue making our lunch – on the basis that you shouldn't make decisions on an empty stomach! Lin filled up the kettle and when the cooker, a regular trangia camping stove, refused to light after its dunking, I dug out the spare burner that I'd literally just found while tidying the bow cabin. In a strange way it felt like we were following a predefined script as the day unfolded. I carried on rowing and steering while Lin poured boiling water over the meals to rehydrate them, including the errant Cod and Potato! We couldn't quite take it all in and neither of us really felt hungry just then, but we forced some food down anyway, knowing that we needed to keep our strength up then more than ever.

We talked about how to handle the situation and after eating we swapped over. Lin took over on the oars and I headed inside the stern cabin to sort out the bomb-site that our main living quarters had now become. Just the night before we'd had a rather soggy incident when the ocean (a bit too successfully!) tried to join us in bed and consequently all of the mattress pieces had been lifted for drying. These were now jumbled up with flexi-solar panels, clothes, towels, the sat phone, snack food, notebooks and a host of other bits and pieces. I sat down with the hatch firmly closed behind me and started hunting for the phone. After I dug it out from underneath a pile of stuff, I called Tony our Duty Officer at race control in the UK. We'd already spoken to him earlier that day to tell him how extreme the conditions were and that it was making us quite nervous. Although he obviously couldn't change the conditions for us, he was normally pretty good at boosting our confidence. We always felt better after talking to him, but I wondered how this second call was going to be received.

As it turned out, it was probably the most exciting point of the race for our Duty Officer. When I explained what had just happened, a deafening "WOW! Really? That's amazing! Was it a full 360 degrees? What happened? Did the boat self right? Were you both in the cabin? You know you're the only boat to capsize so far this year? Are you both OK?" followed!

Of course, we weren't too proud of being the only boat to capsize, it was really embarrassing (cue comments about women drivers!), although right then we were just relieved to be in one piece. Before the call Lin and I had discussed our options and we'd already decided that we didn't need assistance. But we did agree to ask whether the support yacht could turn back to pay us a morale boosting visit. Not surprisingly I was gutted to hear that the crew were already in Antigua and it would take too long for them to beat their way upwind and back out to us. It was a real disappointment and just highlighted the feeling of being on our own and isolated. As we'd expected, once Tony had established the facts around our capsize, he did offer us the option of a rescue, which we turned down. We knew that if we did need help of any kind it was just a phone call away and the reality was that life onboard was already pretty much back to normal. Even so, I finished the call feeling quite low and emotional.

I went back outside to report the conversation to Lin and we chatted about what we wanted to do next. Having already run through possibility of being rescued before making the call to Tony, we'd agreed as a team that we wanted to carry on and there was no need to rely on others for help. Giving up at this stage just wasn't an option as we were less than 300 miles from the finish. Shaken up we might be, but physically we were fine, the boat was fine, and quite simply we were both too stubborn to give up after all we'd been through to get that far.

We called Tony again later on and explained our plan to go onto sea anchor that night to give ourselves a breather. It meant that we wouldn't be moving much and we didn't want him to worry when he saw our progress slow down overnight. We also confirmed with him that we didn't want to tell our families about the capsize. We knew they were excitedly gearing up for their trip to Antigua and news like that would cause immeasurable stress for them. As they couldn't do anything to help, there really was no need for them to know about it until we were safely on dry land.

By the evening we both felt exhausted, drained and empty. We were in uncharted emotional territory and figuring things out as we went along. Seeing the crew from Kilcullen, our support yacht, would have given us a huge boost and just made the feeling of being alone all the more apparent. Whatever happened next was purely down to us, and how we chose to react to the situation. We really didn't want to give up and had quickly dismissed the idea, but there was no question that we'd had a bit of a scare and the last stretch of our race was going to be tough.

Lin had already had a bit of a cry to release the tension of the situation and I knew I needed to as well, but the adrenaline was still flowing and I struggled to let it go. Eventually Lin suggested that I open the special '999' card from my partner Paul – for use only in an emergency. As she pointed out, if right then didn't count as an emergency, then she really didn't know what would! Sure enough, reading the words Paul had written proved to be the catalyst I needed, and feeling much better after a few tears, I took my next turn at the oars.

That night we put the sea anchor out as dusk drew in and ate dinner together inside our now exceptionally tidy cabin! We treated ourselves to our favourite food and drank the mini bottle of champagne we'd been saving to celebrate passing the 300 miles to go mark, and while we could have settled for a low mood, we forced ourselves to laugh at the situation. It was ludicrous, the two of us bobbing around in the water with our dinner floating past! We joked about Neptune trying on his new trendy Bolle sunglasses, and the stylish whale that must now be sporting our loo lid as a flat cap! A good dose of comedy on the iPod helped us to settle down for the night, the laughter being a great remedy and helping to put things into a degree of perspective!

We did decide to tell one other person about the capsize though, and emailed Debra Searle late in the evening. Debra was a dragon boat racing team-mate of ours, who completed the row alone in 2001/02 when her then husband was famously taken off their boat after developing a phobia of the ocean. Debra had first put the idea to us to take part in the race and had continued to encourage us all the way through. We knew that she was the one person in the world who would understand how we were feeling and would know exactly what to say to help us pick ourselves up, ready to continue our battle.

We were right. Debra texted straight back and she truly did understand. Her emotion laced messages reminded us that we are all able to cope with far more mental and physical hardship than we ever imagine. We may feel out of control of a situation or event, but we should take back control of what we can – and that control is choosing how to respond.

We knew that she was right, and our 'movie', the little films or metaphors running inside our minds did not and would not finish in this way. Our race was not going to be over until we stepped onto dry land exactly as we'd pictured it in the months and years running up to the challenge. We thought about that moment; the looks of pride on our loved ones faces, the things we would say to them and how the first hug would feel. We just had to get through the next few days. In the bigger picture, what we felt then was nothing, while that incredible moment would be everything.

We slept surprisingly well that night and by morning were full of fresh, if a little shaky resolve, ready for the task ahead. With more than a little trepidation, we hauled in the sea anchor together, as solid a team as we'd ever been, and prepared to start rowing. We'd barely moved in the night, just 6 miles west and 1 mile south. But the goal was very definitely to get to Antigua – as fast as possible and the right way up! As the sun painted streaks of colour across the morning sky, it was business as usual on the Antigua Express.

Chapter 2

It would be natural to assume that I came from a relatively sporting family, but that's definitely not the case. Being rather short and with a tendency to the 'curvy' side, I showed little aptitude for school sports. I wasn't bad at hitting things, such as in tennis or rounders, but I could barely stumble to the school gates without wheezing to a stop on cross country runs and I was truly awful at anything where height is an advantage, such as netball! I later found out that the horrible breathlessness I suffered then was probably due to asthma that went undetected until I was at college.

From the earliest time I can remember, I was obsessed with horses and Mum still claims that 'horse' was the first word I uttered. Being brought up in a tiny country village for my first four years, there were plenty of equines of all shapes and sizes around to keep my attention and I would shoot to the window at the merest hint of hooves on the road outside. It was only when I was nine that Mum found out the 'pony' my baby sitter Sash took me to ride as a 3-year old toddler was actually a Shire horse! I think she knew for sure then that I was going to be trouble.

Despite the roaring fire behind, at one year old I clearly loved
the paddling pool I got for Christmas!

My Dad was a minister, so we moved round quite a bit when I was growing up, but eventually settled in and around St Helens in the North West. There was never much money to spare and despite writing detailed lists to Father Christmas every autumn, the horse of my dreams never quite made it down the chimney. Instead I devoted myself to saving up my pocket money all year round, so that I could afford riding lessons and pony trekking on our annual family holidays to Pembrokeshire. I read every book I could find and watched every programme to pick up information about horses and looking back it was perhaps an early indication of how doggedly determined I would turn out to be!

Those family holidays also revealed another fascination – the sea! We'd pack up our caravan and drive overnight, parking up at the beach in the early morning. While Mum cooked breakfast on the camping stove, I could normally be found racing down to the sea, impatient to get in the freezing water even at 7am. Surfing was just taking off in the UK then and I bought a 'surf board' of sorts and played for hours in the water. I loved the feeling of gliding along with the waves. Mum hates the water and won't go deeper than her ankles, but Dad used to wade out through the big breakers with me, to the point when I was well out of my depth, but he was there to make sure I was OK.

With Dad on the beach
circa 1972

And with my much loved
surf board!

I loved reading and devoured books as if they were going out of fashion, something that has never changed. Enid Blyton stories most appealed to my vivid imagination and I longed to be a member of the Famous Five or Secret Seven and have amazing adventures like they did. I used to spend hours playing outside with my brother and my cousins when they came to visit, finding new hiding places and sometimes running through the grounds of a nearby school to see the horses in the field at the end of our road. I was fearless enough then to sit on them bareback, not

17

even knowing whether they were trained to be ridden; all the time keeping a sharp eye open for their owners!

In the school holidays we used to go off on our bikes in the morning, returning home only when we were hungry. Or walking home from school I'd get distracted by the old Blacksmith round the corner shoeing a horse and forget to go home. Sometimes my brother and I would disappear for so long that Mum would have to come out hunting for us and a sharp clip around the ear generally preceded any dinner!

I did get bullied at school. If your Dad is a minister, it's really not cool. Especially if he is friends with the headmaster and comes to your school to conduct harvest festivals and Christmas assembly services in front of your classmates. Along with the moving around, changing school, an unusual middle name and the height issue, it instantly made me different at a time when being the same and fitting in was so important. I found the best way to discourage the bullying was never to rise to it, so if my books were tipped all over the floor, I'd just pick them back up quietly. I spent a lot of time desperately trying to fit in and my school reports generally read 'quiet and conscientious', which was a far cry from the bright, chatty and bubbly child everyone knew outside the school gates.

By senior school I'd decided that all I wanted to do was work with horses. But as there was no chance of getting one, or being able to afford lessons, all of my theoretical knowledge was going to waste. I'd seen a farm from the school bus that always had horses outside, and with a little prompting, found out the owners name and wrote to her to ask if I could work there at the weekends.

So, at the age of 13, I had my first interview and got a Saturday job... mucking out. I loved it! The horses were beautiful Arabians, the stuff of little girls' dreams and I used to cycle the 12 mile round trip twice a day to make the most of my time around them. I spent all of my spare time amongst my four-legged friends and this job led to others, including 3 years looking after Emma Hindle's ponies. Now an Olympic dressage rider, Emma is a great example that having wealth doesn't buy success, you still have to work hard, maybe even harder than others, to get to the top.

Pony trekking during our summer holidays

Teenage years are always a little tempestuous, but for me they brought something that would change life forever. I didn't actually want to write about this, as I rarely talk about it and only my closest friends know – but my brother convinced me to include it in this book because he thinks it explains a lot about me. You see, when I was 14 and my brother was 10 our Dad disappeared. Literally. One day he went out and simply never came back.

On that terrible day, it started with mild worry that he was late for dinner, then as the hours went by, the police got involved. His behaviour was so out of character, and he was so well known in the area that he was registered as a missing person immediately. Life quickly became a living horror story. Our car was found a few days later with no sign of Dad, and bar a few unconfirmed sightings around the UK, he was never seen again.

The reason I don't like to talk about this part of my life because I've learnt that the reaction it generates in others is fairly predictable and I don't handle it well. There's instant sympathy (which makes me uncomfortable) as you'd get for bereavement, but then the real magnitude of what a missing person means sinks in – and the questions start. How can someone just disappear like that? Was he ever seen again? Did he ever try to make contact? Do you think he left the country? Why did he leave? Do you think he's still alive? Plus a hundred and one others.

Unfortunately I don't have the answers and probably never will now. Over time, as we pieced things together, we worked out that he'd been involved in a business venture that had gone horribly wrong. The debt he'd built up in his efforts to do the right thing we assume eventually led to a breakdown and in a moment of stress, he walked away. The longer he was away, the harder it was to come back home. And that's it really.

Once people know, they tend to view you differently and I don't want to be treated with sympathy all the time – worse things do happen after all. So I generally find it easier to tell people that I 'lost' my father when I was young and that seems to do the trick!

The thing is, if someone close to you dies, it's devastating, but there's a recognised grieving process to go through. It's different for everyone, but we all understand it and know it needs to take place. When someone close to you disappears, there is no process. You can't grieve and gain 'closure' because they haven't died, or at least you don't know for sure. Sometimes you never find out. Even though Dad was declared legally dead some years later, his entire extended family are left hanging on, never knowing whether they might walk past him in the street, whether he'll track us down and turn up on the doorstep, or whether the next body uncovered somewhere might be his. I know that sounds dramatic, but that's just how it is. A never ending nightmare.

Looking back, I guess this made me grow up quickly and I learnt to be independent very early on. I tried hard not to be a burden to Mum and learnt to live with the uncertainty, being singled out as different because of it, along with the rollercoaster of hope and despair that comes with the territory. Of course it fades in time as you find a way to accept and live with it. Nowadays psychologists probably have a field day with the emotional side of coping with a missing person, but help of that kind simply wasn't available back then.

I'm sure this upheaval did impact on my performance at school, and I think I was a big disappointment to my teachers. I never enjoyed it – and it definitely wasn't the happiest time of my life. I just couldn't see the point of learning about things I wasn't interested in. I had no aspirations to go to university and felt over awed by the many class-mates who got into Oxford or Cambridge. Instead I stuck to my guns and despite discouragement from school, kept planning my equestrian ambitions.

I did decide to stay on into sixth form where there was far more independence and I actually enjoyed those two years; we were allowed to wear our own clothes and once we had driving licences, we could pinch our parents' cars and drive to school. I took mostly sciences, Biology, Geography and Geology, although we all had to suffer General Studies as well.

Playing in my white water boat

We had a new range of sports options that we could choose from for our Wednesday afternoon entertainment and I picked kayaking as I'd done some before on activity holidays in the Lake District and on the Norfolk Broads and enjoyed it. I distinctly remember my first kayaking experience, and it wasn't good when I ended up spinning around in the middle of Lake Windermere on my own, struggling against the wind to get back to the activity centre. Despite that, I tried again on the Broads boating holidays and seemed to figure it out. Apparently being small but quite strong (probably from all that mucking out!) can be an advantage in paddle sports.

I joined the school canoe club, run by an international paddler and Biology teacher, Dave Bangs. Dave lived for paddling, and as we normally went out of school to do white water runs, or longer river and lake trips, we got to miss the dreaded General Studies! I took to the sport very quickly and although scared stiff by rapids, actually ran some fairly large rivers in a variety of boats. Of course we all fell in sometimes and I've had a touch of hypothermia more than once, but we always had the right training, safety equipment and cover for what we were doing. It was a good habit to get into.

Around that time, Dave got involved in a sport called dragon boat racing and because he was involved, inevitably we were too. There was a nice group of us who paddled regularly and I loved being 'one of the lads'. When we got asked to go dragon boat racing, and found out that it meant weekends away without our parents, of course we jumped at the chance. Again I took to the sport quickly and loved the team ethos, but had no idea back then how big a part of my life dragon boat racing was to become.

I left school and home at 18, moving to Yorkshire to follow my dream and work with horses in an eventing yard. We broke horses in and specialised in sorting out problem equines, and boy did we get some nutters! But mostly they were just a bit spoiled and needed a couple of weeks of firm handling to bring them back into line. Life was different there though. I shared my boss's cottage and worked from 7am to 6pm every day. The cottage had no central heating and I was only allowed to use the electric heater for an hour each morning and night, so with ice often forming on the inside of the windows, I slept in more layers than I worked in. Consequently, I'd now count myself as an expert in lighting open fires!

My favourite horse in Yorkshire, and probably the fastest - Chilac

As a working pupil, I didn't get paid but Mum sent me £10 a week and I took on 3 part time jobs to make ends meet. Days were incredibly long and if we had horses competing, my working day could run from 3am to the early hours of the following morning, so I often survived on minimal sleep. I also worked 7 days a week, saving up my days off so that I could go home every few weeks for a proper break.

It was hard, dirty work, but I loved it. I adored the horses that I looked after and we had a lot of fun in the year that I was there. I also learnt a lot about myself, not all of which was positive as I recognised feelings of intense frustration when I lost out on riding tuition due to not having my own horse. I was never as good a rider as I wanted to be, so I poured my effort into studying. It paid off though and I actually did go to university in the end – to study equine science of course!

I thoroughly enjoyed university and certainly made the most of being away from home and living a student life. I had to complete two work placements during the 3-year course and for the first spent a wonderful summer working for a lovely family in Italy. It was certainly a challenge but I coped well in a country where I didn't speak the language, where very scary, mutant-sized insects roamed free and the cat brought in snakes instead of mice! I got to ride and care for some fabulous horses including one who competed at the Seoul Olympics. But returning to the UK it took me a long time to settle back into my studies, and when the next placement came round I applied for jobs further afield.

Riding a dressage test in Chicago...

I ended up heading west to Chicago and worked in a large riding school and livery yard for almost a year. Again I loved my job and had some wonderful clients who I'm still in contact with. But I also had a troublesome boss who suffered from terrible mood swings. My accommodation was awful and a lack of transport made life very difficult sometimes. Nonetheless, I worked hard and even if the boss was never happy, I gained a huge amount of respect from the clients and from visiting Grand Prix riders. It was my first Christmas away from home and the whole year was tough, both physically and mentally, but I came away with the knowledge that I could be pretty resilient and resourceful when I needed to be.

23

…and the ribbons that Fanfare and I won!

Back home disaster struck and in my last term I had a bad fall. Falling off is part and parcel of a life with horses, and I have hit the ground more times than I can actually remember, but normally bounced back with no more than a bruised ego. I'd damaged my back and neck badly a couple of years before and this fall resulted in another trip to hospital. This time I fell sideways out of the saddle while cross country jumping and literally tore my right knee apart. Despite barely being able to stand (let alone get back on the horse), as the shock kicked in I managed to drive 40 miles home to safety, where I knew someone would be able to get me to hospital. But it was a long route to recovery and many years later resulted in surgery.

I graduated in the spectacular surrounding of Coventry Cathedral and moved on to a teaching job closer to home. It was a great job and I quickly built up a strong customer group and a successful little business. But the horse world does seem to have more than its fair share of crooks; and I came to the slow conclusion that this family were more crooked than most. I stayed for a year, overworked myself straight to a dose of pneumonia (not ideal when you are asthmatic!) and narrowly escaped before I got too mixed up in a lifestyle and situation that I didn't want to be involved in. The day I left was frightening but it was definitely the right move, and I was so ill by then that I couldn't have continued anyway.

I felt that I needed time to recover and ended up taking a telesales job for a company called NWS Bank, discovering that my inherently chatty nature was ideal for the role! A few months later I put forward an idea for a new product and was moved into marketing to develop and launch the product – Equine Finance! It was never a best seller, but I got a huge sense of satisfaction from seeing my idea grow and take shape.

Better still, the more regular hours meant that I could take up kayaking again, which then led to dragon boat racing once more. A whole new world of training, racing and international events opened up and there was plenty of opportunity for travel, meeting new people, socialising and romance. Life was good!

Chapter 3

Lin and I first met in 1994 when I moved into the Marketing department at Bank of Scotland (then NWS Bank) and it was Lin's own love of horses that first got us talking. We became firm friends straight away, discovering that we had a lot in common and this friendship has turned out to be the most enduring for both of us.

Tempted by the lure of 'we're going to the World Championships in China next year, would you like to come?' I started to train regularly (well, three times a week!) with the dragon boat club on the basis that I'd never been to China and I thought it would be pretty cool to represent Great Britain. I had to take on a second job as a Bettaware salesperson in order to raise the money to go - dragon boat racing was and still is a self-funded sport, right up to international level.

In 1995, I travelled to an obscure part of China to compete in the first ever, official World Championships. Getting there took 2 days and involved some interesting travel companions, mostly of the cockroach kind. Being there was a strange experience – we were treated as celebrities because in China being a dragon boat paddler is a great thing to be, rather than just a slightly odd hobby as it's viewed in the UK! The opening ceremony was a wash out, but attended by tens of thousands of local people, many of who had paid huge sums to get a ticket. We were largely kept away from the locals by the police, although many people brought their children to see the foreigners, and if we were wearing team kit, drivers would stop their cars to allow us to cross the normally crazy roads in safety.

I learnt a lot about preparation for a big event that week, not least because China's master plan to win seemed to involve a good dose of food poisoning (I'll skip the details!) for the foreign teams. I was gutted to miss the 1,000m event due to illness, but recovered in time for the 500m and 250m Mixed races – we didn't have a women's team that year. Racing was hard, the heat and humidity in Yue Yang were outrageous and unforgiving, and I remember lining up for the minor final (which decides places 6-10) of the 500m race on the last baking hot day, literally gasping for breath before we even started.

With the boats locked into the start pontoon, the sun beat down on us and the atmosphere was electric. We were ready, the start sounded and we were off. As we ploughed the heavy teak boat down the course, straining with the effort, we clawed our way past the USA team and crossed the line to take 9th place. I just couldn't believe it! As I sat up in the boat and looked around I realised that we'd just made a little bit of history and finished inside the top ten in the whole World – in single figures! It was an incredible high, and I suddenly knew that I wanted to carry on and do more with this sport, finish higher up in the rankings, and that a medal might not be out of my grasp after all!

Back home, Lin was fascinated by my stories of dragon boat racing and keen to join in when she heard that my club, Amathus, was planning to start up a new women's team. The first training session could have gone better though; it poured with rain from start to finish, great, vertical, stair rods of rain that really hurt! But Lin was hooked from that day on, and after her first race in Cardiff a few weeks later; dragon boat racing had acquired a new follower.

I took Lin along to a Great Britain squad training session in 1996 although she was convinced that reaching the standard for the team was beyond her. But during the session something changed. She realised that everyone else there was really just like her, and that representing her country could be a very real possibility. After all, if they could do it, why shouldn't she be able to?

The Great Britain squad and team structure was fully introduced into the UK in 1997, and with it came the horror that is 'Time Trials'. These are individual trials in a one person boat to determine the fastest combination of 20 paddlers in the UK. Lin and I trained together for the trials and both made it onto the team for the warm up event in Macau and the World Championships in Hong Kong. That summer we spent endless hours driving from Chester to London for team training and it was a time when we got to know each other inside out, had a lot of laughs, shared our dreams and fears and developed our lasting friendship. I still remember the day our new GB kit arrived too, shiny lycra suits in red, white and blue, and the excitement we felt as we tried them on in the bright sunshine and danced around like loons!

We shared a room in Macau for our warm up event and got on really well, supporting each other through the anxiety and stress of racing at this level. We seemed to naturally understand when the other one needed a bit of space, a bit of a giggle, or just a hug! Racing took place in a typhoon shelter in an extremely strong wind – which bent the palm trees double and felt like paddling into the mouth of a hairdryer on the hot setting. But we had to laugh at the toilets – which were simply a couple of planks missing from the floor of a hut built over the water. When the tide was in, the fishes got a feast and when it was out you could aim for the little crabs scuttling around on the sand! Amazingly, and despite some 'tactical' starts from the far East crews (who like to set off before the man says 'Go'!), we won both of our races that weekend.

Celebrating in Macau after winning both of our races.

At the celebration dinner after the event, the GB Women received a standing ovation from the other paddlers, enjoyed a sumptuous feast and ended the evening by conga-ing round the room with the Mayor of Macau! But that night was also memorable because we first met Pam Newby. Pam was the helm (sweep) for the South African team and had struggled to keep their boat on line in the strong wind. We bumped into her as she sobbed in a doorway after another team member had been particularly scathing about her ability to control the boat, something that we felt was an unfair accusation.

Immediately we stepped in to help, with Lin announcing that there was nothing wrong with losing control of a boat, it happens to everyone who helms at some time or another. In fact wasn't it only a few weeks since I had stuffed Britain's number one men's crew into the bank halfway down the course? It was true, if embarrassing, and we both hugged Pam and took her inside for a drink and a bit of confidence building, Lin and Rachel style! Later on, we made Pam a friendship bracelet to wear in Hong Kong to bring her luck – and she had no further steering problems!

Once in Hong Kong we found there were some issues with the GB team dynamics and the two of us stuck together more than ever in order to distance ourselves from some of our more neurotic team-mates who seemed to believe other athletes were trying to intimidate us. It was unsettling for the whole team and we just couldn't understand it as we loved meeting competitors from the other countries and seemed to thrive on the big event atmosphere. OK, so the Germans did have hairy armpits and were huge, somewhat manly women, but there was the pride of Great Britain at stake here. And sharing a bathroom with the American men proved to be no REAL hardship for us!

Our team target for this World Championships was to make it into the major finals in each distance – this decides first to sixth place. In the 1,000m we did make it to the final, and although we came last, the reality was that 6th place was a dream come true. In the 250m we were really fired up as we fought through the rounds and again lined up on the start to take our place in the final. At this point, what seemed to be a solid wall of water moved down the course towards us, and when it hit we had to bend over double in the boat because the rain really hurt! But with a British stiff upper lip and some rapid bailing, we raced our hearts out to move up a place into 5th. We also managed 5th in the 500m event, just 3 seconds off a bronze medal. And all of a sudden it became clear. If we could train harder and go 3 seconds faster, individually and as a team, then we'd be in the medals next time! The effect on us was like dangling a big, juicy carrot – and I desperately wanted to experience standing on the podium, maybe even hearing the National Anthem, and receive a medal one day soon.

For the European Championships in Rome the following year we had an extremely strong team and one of the new members was a girl called Debra Newbury. Debra proved to be an exceptional team member and I remember her telling us all about her amazing plans to row across the Atlantic following her wedding to Andrew Veal. I had qualified to race in both the Mixed and Women's teams and we took our competition to a new level, returning with 2 silver and 2 bronze medals. I couldn't believe that I'd actually done it and won medals while representing Great Britain. Going up to collect them with the team and seeing the Union Flag hoisted was without doubt the proudest moment of my life.

A rare picture of us with Debra (in the hat).
I'm behind her to the left, talking to Lin who is directly behind Debra.

But the funniest part of this trip was our skit of the Spice Girls at the closing party or 'cultural display'. We get a bit stuck on cultural displays in the UK as our traditional Morris Dancing just doesn't really cut it when compared to African tribal dancing or a New Zealand Haka! Somehow, Lin ended up as Baby Spice, while I was Ginger Spice – those curves do come in useful occasionally! Debra had choreographed a routine for us, together with our friend Karen (Sporty) and the two biggest Royal Marines we could find from the men's team transformed into Scary and Posh. Our act brought the house down and was the talk of the dragon boat world for years to come, but luckily the photos are few and far between!!

With a taste of glory behind me, my sights were firmly set on Gold medals and I dearly wanted to hear the National Anthem played for the GB team. So it was back to training for the Worlds which were to be held in the far less glamorous location of... Nottingham! Hosting the event did however allow us to train on the already familiar course, which had to be a bonus. Working with our coach 'Griff', we introduced new techniques such as visualisation, to keep the team focused and strong and we found they worked really well. I was the stroke paddler this time round and my responsibility was to set the paddling rate for the whole team throughout the race. I found it hard to handle this additional stress which played on my nerves and the challenge was to find new ways to deal with it.

Nerves make me feel sick and one of the best pieces of advice I've received was not to fight it but to accept the feeling. Horrible though it is, feeling sick with nerves is normal for me and I should really only worry if the feeling isn't there. So, with motivating music, walking out my race, visualisation, centreing, breathing exercises and sunglasses to hide my tears of sheer terror on the way to the start, I got through the races and returned home inspired with a silver and two bronze medals. We crossed paths with our South African friend Pam again as she was in Nottingham that year, wearing her friendship bracelet, and was still wearing it with pride when I stayed at her home a few months later while racing in Cape Town.

Cape Town – Pam helming and I'm front right

At future events our results continued to be extremely strong and I believe this is purely down to the quality of coaching from our women's team guru, John 'Griff' Griffiths, combined with the dedication of the women who train with the squad and the final selected team. Although it kept eluding us at World Championships, we won Gold several times at European competitions, and I always enjoy the incredible experience of standing proud and hearing our National Anthem played. Of course I'm normally in tears by the end of the first line!

It wasn't all success though, and a 4th place in the 1,000m in Philadelphia (2001) on the first day of racing brought us down to earth with a bump, especially as we had a really strong team and that was supposed to be our best event. Fourth is the worst possible place to be really – all that effort and not a thing to show for it. So picking ourselves back up again to continue the fight was a tricky thing to do. Under Griff's guidance the team managed to put the disappointing result behind them and really pulled together to go on and win bronze in both our other races.

Philadelphia - GB Women in Lane 2, Bronze medal position.
I'm third from the front.

In 2003 the World Championships were moved from Shanghai due to fears surrounding the SARS virus outbreak. The alternative venue chosen was Poznan in Poland, where we'd previously performed extremely well at European Championships, even setting a new record for the Women's 1,000m.

I'd been lucky enough by then to have received some coaching from David Hemery, the 400m hurdler who won Gold in the 1968 Olympics. One point that really stuck with me was when David told us that if all the technical pieces were in place, you just have to believe in yourself. Well, we'd trained harder than ever before and the team was without doubt the strongest ever, although it had been a really tough year for me as Paul had spent 6 months in Iraq at the start of the war. This emotional trauma, combined with ongoing shoulder and back injuries really affected my ability to train and I qualified lower down the ranking than ever before – but I knew deep down that it's better to be a slow paddler in a strong team, than a fast paddler in a weak one! I really believed that this was our year and as we paddled to the start, I knew that the pieces were in place. I had 'that feeling'.

I remember sitting on the start line and looking down the

length of the course to the finish markers. The knowledge that in just over 4 minutes I would either be a World Champion, or the most disappointed person on the planet, was overwhelming and at that exact moment I would rather have been anywhere else in the world than in that boat. I'd somehow got it into my head that I might miss the start, although I've never missed a start in my life. So I concentrated hard, running the start sequence over and over in my head, seeing, feeling and hearing it - blocking everything else out. 'Are you ready, Attention, Go! Are you ready, Attention, Go!

A couple of tears squeezed out as I went through my normal preparations, sitting tall, breathing exercises and visualisation, all the time shaking so hard that my paddle rattled on the gunwales of the boat. It was too hard to take in and too big to comprehend, but it really was now, or never. This was my one chance and I might never get another opportunity. I played the words of Eminem's song *'Lose yourself'* in my head:

"Look, if you had one shot, one opportunity
To seize everything you ever wanted? One moment
Would you capture it or just let it slip?"

We all had to seize this opportunity in both hands and as the man said 'go', the team shot out of the start pontoons like a bullet out of a gun. I didn't miss the start! Together we called on every part of our accumulated experience to get that boat down the course in the fastest possible time. I had never paddled so hard in my entire life and I know without question that the same could be said for each team member. The race plan went like clockwork and we started to pull away, inch by inch, stroke by stroke, seat by seat. The team committed and together we reached out and took our prize from the other teams. We knew that we wanted it more and if anyone else tried, it was going to hurt them to take it away from us.

In the final 250m we could sense the crowds' anticipation, but we also knew that we were already in front, we just had to stay there. I couldn't breathe, couldn't see and couldn't hear. All my effort was going into each paddle stroke, making it solid, strong and in time. Our last 10 strokes were amazing and as we crossed the line our heads went up. The nearest boat was half a length away – almost unheard of at this level of competition – and we were in front. We'd done it, really done it! At last we'd won that elusive Gold medal and smashed our own World Record into the bargain.

Winning World Gold in Poznan in a World Record time.
I'm third from the front of the boat.

Shortly after the finish, we brought the boat in to a rapturous welcome from the GB teams and the other countries. But what was really special for me was that Paul had made it back safely from Iraq in time to come and share that amazing moment. Pam was there too, with her friendship bracelet, waiting to welcome us in and congratulate us.

I felt 10 feet tall (I'm actually only 5'1"!) as I stood on the podium to receive that special medal. It was and always will be one of the most treasured and precious items that I own. I breathed in the fantastic feeling of being part of a team who are the best in the World, absorbing every moment of the experience.

When I eventually came back down to earth again I decided to take 2004 off and sort out the old niggling knee injury that required quite serious surgery. I'd worked for so long to get that medal and I needed a bit of time to reflect and think about the future.

With the elusive World Gold medal in Poznan 2003.

I went back to dragon boat racing briefly in 2005, helming for the GB Women's team at the World Championships in Berlin. Helming is truly terrifying as it's the only position where any problem or mistake is immediately and publicly apparent. I was incredibly nervous about carrying such a huge responsibility and the hopes and dreams of my team, and I had to work hard to manage my own emotions without affecting the paddlers.

But just before our first practice, Pam appeared unexpectedly – I didn't even know she was in the country – and placed the friendship bracelet on my wrist, loaning it to me for the event to bring me good luck! It was ironic as we'd only met because of helming in the first place! It must have worked though; I steered straight and true in every race, helping my team to a silver and two bronze medals.

Dragon boat racing is an intriguing and addictive sport and over the years Lin and I both learnt a lot that would later help us to cope with rowing across the Atlantic.

Helming in Berlin 2005.

From the meticulous preparations and attention to detail to the tolerance and understanding of your team mates; the discipline and dedication to the visualisation and other techniques that help make the fraction of a second difference between winning and losing. Plus the support we received from the dragon boat racing community around the world. Without all of that, I'm not sure that we would have been quite as well prepared or successful as we were.

Chapter 4

While Lin and I were busily absorbed in pursuing our dragon boat racing careers, Debra had set off to take part in the 2001 Atlantic Rowing Race. We'd got to know her and Andrew reasonably well through her time on the GB team and consequently followed their progress with great interest.

We were soon horrified to hear that Andrew had to be taken off the boat after just a few days when he developed a phobia of the open space of the ocean and simply couldn't continue. Debra meanwhile was enjoying the challenge and with Andrew's support, decided to carry on alone. 111 days later, she rowed triumphantly into Barbados, making headline news, having completed the arduous journey solo. Although the crossing had been incredibly tough, Debra had bravely stuck it out and this awesome experience ultimately led to her taking a new career path as a professional adventurer.

I clearly remember the day I stopped by to chat with Debra while I was working at the Southampton Boat Show. Her boat, Troika, was there and I was really moved by the video footage of her time onboard. I bought her newly released book, reading it over and over again, but much as I dreamt about rowing the ocean, I just couldn't see any way to fund a project of that size, so I kept the thoughts to myself and concentrated on dragon boat racing.

Lin was equally captivated by the story and did talk about giving it a go, never really expecting it to become anything other than a dream. But every time I saw Debra she suggested that I should think about the Atlantic Race. In her opinion I was the right kind of person to take it on and she thought I'd enjoy it, and let's face it – she should know! She had also had similar conversations with Lin. By chance, an acquaintance of Lin's was planning to take part in the 2005 race and was looking for a partner and although Lin did approach me first, it just wasn't the right time for me to get involved, so Lin jumped at the chance and decided to enter the race.

All too soon though it became apparent that this was completely the wrong partnership and it was unlikely that as a team they were even going to make the start line. Communication was not smooth and the male/female pairing brought additional stresses, leading Lin to confess that she thought it just wasn't going to work. I meanwhile, was having a terrible time at work and not enjoying it at all which prompted me to take a good, hard look at life in general. Maybe I was just unable to settle after the Worlds, or maybe I should have moved on to a new challenge professionally. Either way, something wasn't right.

I saw Debra, again at the Southampton Boat Show, in September 2004 and once more she suggested that I consider the row. This time I thought it through a bit more. I mentioned it to Paul, but he laughed about it and brushed it to one side. So I thought some more. Surely if Debra had managed to get across alone, then Lin and I would stand a fighting change of doing it between us? Why shouldn't I be able? What was really stopping me from following this particular dream? Was it the money? Was I too scared? Not strong enough? Or just not quite determined enough to make my family proud?

Lin and I had talked a lot over the years about getting involved in a fundraising challenge of some kind. We had looked into a number of treks, cycle rides and the like, but hadn't found anything that really (pardon the pun) floated our boat! In particular we wanted to do something for a breast cancer charity due to the massive impact it has had on both our lives by affecting family members and friends. I lost my grandmother to breast cancer when I was quite young and Lin lost her mother-in-law much more recently, so it is genuinely something close to our hearts.

All of a sudden it became clear. The light bulb went on and the penny dropped! Quite simply there was absolutely no reason why we shouldn't be able to do the race. We were physically and mentally capable, and it would provide the perfect platform for us to raise a huge amount of money for a charity, possibly even covering the costs of taking part if we set things up the right way.

On a dreary November day, I remember sitting in Lin's living room. I can still picture the dim autumn light filtering through the windows and tiny dust motes floating in the air. It was one of those times when you know that what you are about to say is going to change your life forever. Once it's out you can't take it back and you know it will alter the status quo and send you off on a completely new tangent... but you're still going to say it anyway. I took deep breath and asked Lin how preparations for her row were going. The answer was "They're not!" My chance had come.

In a roundabout sort of way, I asked whether she might consider doing the row with someone else... like me? She jumped at the opportunity, 'Is that a 'yes' then?'

I still don't think I actually did say 'yes' that day, or on any day following! But at the time it was immaterial and the deal was done. Straight away we decided that we should be able to make the start of the 2007 race, three years away, and that the first charity we wanted to approach was Breast Cancer Care.

Lin made the first contact with Breast Cancer Care and we were invited in to meet the team and discuss our ideas. We carefully constructed a presentation, which aimed to prove that we were sensible, professional women with a valid proposition, rather than a pair of lunatics with some harebrained scheme that was bound to fail. Some would say it was a tough call!

The presentation took three exhausting hours and they questioned us on every aspect of our plans. The only question we couldn't give a good answer on was 'so what happens if the only publicity we get is an upturned boat and two dead rowers?' Um, they'd kinda got us on that one! All we could do was be as realistic as possible and assure them that while we couldn't guarantee that it wouldn't happen, it was in our best interests too, for obvious reasons (like staying alive) that we try to avoid that particular outcome at all costs!

A week later we received a phone call to confirm that we could represent Breast Cancer Care for our rowing challenge with their blessing and support. Our professionalism, knowledge and enthusiasm had won them over and we'd even pipped another, more experienced crew (Rowgirls) to the post as they had also approached Breast Cancer Care with a similar proposition. Our first goal had been achieved and the project was underway!

Chapter 5

I had decided not to tell Paul about the challenge until we had confirmed Breast Cancer Care's support but now we had that confirmation, the deed had to be done. To say it went down badly would be an understatement, and breaking the news caused tears and harsh words. Tears on my part, and harsh words (in my opinion) on his part.

Paul simply couldn't understand why I would put myself in such great danger when there were so many other options out there for adventures and fundraising. At the time he was in the Royal Marines and simply wouldn't accept my argument that his situation was just the same. His get out clause was 'but that's my job and you don't have to do the row'. For the first time I realised that I was putting my relationship on the line and it was to become an ongoing issue.

Telling my family was a little easier and I sat down with Mum and my stepfather Wallace, to tell them my plans. Mum's instant reaction was "Well, I think you're bloody stupid". But I guess if we all believed what we were told by others then we'd never do anything! Wallace, as ever, took it all in his stride – as stepfathers go, I couldn't ever ask for better support and he's been there for me, solid as a rock, through so many ups and downs. I hoped he'd talk Mum round for me! A couple of days later Mum phoned me to say that they were looking for crew for the Clipper round the world sailing race and she thought that would be a much safer option! The problem was that Mum had in her mind an image of the kind of open wooden rowing boat you get on a boating lake, but once I showed her a picture of an ocean rowing boat, and talked about the safety side of things she started to understand!

She was also really touched to find out that we were doing the race for a breast cancer charity as it was her own mother, Ivy, who we had lost to the disease some 30 years before. Before long, Mum was well on the way to becoming a 'super-supporter'!

My brother Gordon was also concerned about the plans, but carefully controlled his desire to panic and asked a lot of questions, based around the safety of the race. Once he was satisfied that I knew what I was talking about and had already considered all of the things he was worried about, he threw himself into the project with us and started to rustle up a merry band of followers in his area.

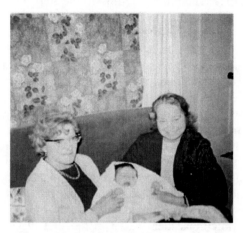

As a baby with both my grandmothers. Ivy is on the right

Work also had to be told, but I completely bottled out of telling my director face to face and approached another member of staff instead. I applied for special leave, which was unpaid and could be approved for up to 18 weeks – but I knew that I had to be prepared for the fact that it might not be possible and I'd have to hand my notice in. So I was thrilled and relieved when James (my director) came back a few days later and told me that he'd arranged for the special leave – but that I was to be paid for the full period. The company couldn't sponsor me directly, but this was his way of showing his support. I couldn't believe it – it was better than I could ever have imagined and meant that I would have far less money worries than I'd anticipated while I was rowing.

Lin had a similar response from her family, but once she'd worked through that, we set a date for our first project meeting. On the Easter weekend of 2005, we sat in Lin's flat surrounded by flip charts, pens and other assorted stationery implements, getting brain ache while we tried to figure out where on earth to start! Sally Kettle (Atlantic 2003 and 2005) had given us a piece of advice passed on to her 'When eating large elephants... take small bites'. So we did.

We split up the challenge into 4 categories – Physical, Mental, Technical and Fundraising/PR, and then listed all the main tasks we would need to complete over the next 3 years under

41

each heading. Having clear goals are important, so we thought about what these should be. Getting to the start line was the first one, along with stepping off in Antigua still as best friends and raising as much money as possible for Breast Cancer Care, but there were other steps to achieving these goals that would give us a good measure of our progress and success. It's all very well having goals, but you need to make sure that you know when you have achieved them!

It was terrifying but incredibly exciting. There was so much to do and so many of the tasks depended on other jobs being done. Getting to the start line depended on, amongst hundreds of other factors, buying a boat, which in turn depended on raising enough money. Raising the money depended on acquiring sponsors, running fundraising events and generating the right sort of PR. What on earth were we thinking? This was a massive challenge and whose ridiculous idea was it in the first place? Debra's of course! As she wasn't there, we decided to blame her anyway!

On the physical side, our first challenge was to learn to row. Despite having tried out most water sports known to man, I had never rowed before and to be honest, I'm not really built for it. Likewise Lin had never tried the sport, but is physically far more suitable. Either way we needed the basics instilled as second nature so that we could avoid injuring ourselves. We actually had our first lessons on the same day; mine at Royal Chester Rowing Club and Lin at Wallbrook in Teddington. On the whole we enjoyed it, managed not to capsize and both ended up racing for our clubs quite early on.

In order to work on endurance we asked Water Rower for help and were both given torture rowing machines to keep at home. This made training a whole lot easier as we could do as much or as little as we had time to do. We gradually built up the time spent on the seat until we could manage a steady 2 hours without difficulty, although the occasional sore butt proved interesting! I combined this with gym work and weights, but confess that they often fell by the wayside as the project went on and we had to balance so many more demands on our time.

Obviously it helps to be a little mental to take on a challenge like this, but in all seriousness, success during the crossing is largely down to your mental strength, tenacity and ability to cope with whatever is thrown at you. Many former rowers advised that it was 95% mental challenge and just 5% physical. We already knew we'd be able to take many techniques from our dragon boat racing careers and decided to see whether Ned Skelton, who we had been coached by before, would be willing to help us with this project. Ned didn't hesitate in saying yes, and we booked our first sessions with great anticipation. In fact Ned ended up getting more involved in the project than any of us had anticipated.

One of our first outings, rowing together.

The technical side of things was a far more daunting prospect. Neither of us is particularly technically minded and there was a lot to take in. Plus, our sea-going experience was pretty much limited to cross-channel ferries and a trip to see a solar eclipse from the water. Neither of us had been out of sight of land on a small boat and although we don't normally get sea sick, the truth was, we'd never really been at sea for long enough to find out if it would be a problem. Yet we took some comfort from other rowers who also had to learn the basics before setting off, but who still made it across the pond. We knew that just as in dragon boat racing, we needed to put the pieces in place and then believe in our ability, both individually and as a team.

We had four mandatory courses to pass in order to qualify for the race, one of which is known to be testing even for experienced mariners. Then we had to learn enough to make sure we bought the right boat, or figure out how to build our own! Added to that was working out what equipment we needed and how to use it, what food and drinks would sustain us and a million and one other small decisions that had to be made, often without really knowing what the best option would be.

Lin's background is Accountancy and mine is Marketing and PR, so we naturally picked up our roles in these areas. We decided straight away that we needed to run our campaign as a 'not-for-profit' company intuitively felt that a highly professional approach (as opposed to the pink and fluffy route) would be our best bet when convincing people that they really, really wanted to give us large (or small) sums of money. It proved to be a good decision!

Although we had the Charity backing, the fundraising was purely down to us and we didn't have a team of willing helpers to sort it out for us. The prospect was terrifying. We worked out the numbers and quaked in our shoes at the line of zero's. Effectively we'd committed to raising the price of a small house, starting from nothing, in just over 2 years. We had no idea if it was even possible, but quickly decided that if we couldn't do it, then no one could! We had to believe it was possible. So we came up with a plan for fundraising and publicising ourselves, decided what we were prepared to do, and detailed the horrifyingly large sum of money we needed to raise each month until the start. Then we had a stiff drink!

Another excellent piece of advice from Sally was to tell everyone and anyone – because you just never know where your next sponsor is going to come from. So we practiced a bit and although we found it hard in the early days, we began to enjoy the reaction it inevitably provoked when you told someone you're going to row the Atlantic. Next we used £60 from our very first sponsor to open a joint account under the name of Atlantic Rowing Challenge. We registered our website address and also registered our entry for the 2007 race with the race organisers, covering the £150 fee ourselves to make it official! Without doubt it was an exciting time, but to be honest, it really felt a little bit like closing our eyes and stepping over the edge of a cliff!

Chapter 6

In September 2005 we both went to the Southampton Boat Show and borrowed space from an electronics company to hold our press launch. Ocean rower Roz Savage was about to set off across the Atlantic and stopped by to show her support, but unfortunately none of the press did! How embarrassing. But towards the end of our time slot, we spotted a couple of unwary reporters wobbling their way from the Guinness Bar to the Champagne Bar – so we accosted them and rescued our dented pride!

Our launch at Southampton Boat Show 2005

Later on I attended a party thrown by Saltwater Communications, the PR experts who had kindly taken us under their wing. I descended on a room full of the Marine industry's great and good, determined to spread the word about naked rowers and fundraising. Certainly knowing most of the journalists helped, and along with copious amounts of alcohol (for them!) I secured a couple of mentions in magazines and a huge amount of interest and offers of support.

The next day was another big day for us. We had arranged to borrow a boat to take part in the Trafalgar Great River Race - 22 miles of rowing down the Thames from Richmond to Greenwich. It was to be our first big test of organisation, endurance and sheer tenacity, as well as the first big fundraiser to kick off our campaign.

The day started off badly (was it a sign?) with locked gates and over zealous security chaps delaying us when we collected the boat. But eventually we saw the boat lifted off the trailer, swinging scarily in the air and onto the water. Soon we too were on the water and ready to go. Our good friend Ned Skelton was in charge of towing, so set off to meet us at the other end, while two friends, Nicky and Jo, were joining us onboard to make up the required number of crew. Wearing pink Breast Cancer Care t-shirts and with the boat decked in balloons we certainly attracted plenty of attention as we lumbered along in our ungainly, rudderless craft.

Partners in crime – before the start!

We rowed against the tide for the first 5 miles, swapping pairs every 30 minutes, and I do remember wondering how on earth we were going to haul a boat like this one all the way across the Atlantic. If I'm honest, I wasn't even sure that I was enjoying the experience at all right then! As the tide turned and started to flow with us, it got a bit easier although steering was problematic all the way. We had a cheeky side wind that day, and with no rudder to help us steer it made it quite hard work, especially when we nearly ended up ramming HMS Belfast!

Towards the end of the race, we were overtaken by a dragon boat team, many of who knew us well. Waving to them, I slipped on the wet deck surface and fell into the deep foot well, grazing my legs quite badly. Bizarrely, it didn't hurt. As I'd just been rowing hard, my body was far more interested in recovering and didn't seem to register the injury, at least until much later, and it looked far worse than it was. But it was a good reminder of how easy it was to get hurt and that injuries could and would happen during the Atlantic crossing.

It took us 4 hours and 17 minutes to get to the finish at Greenwich, and of that time, Lin and I had rowed for around 3 hours together. It was a great feeling to cross the line although the day was far from over. In order to get the boat off the water, we had to cross the river and make for a deep-water mooring – which proved difficult to find. By now the tide was flowing out extremely quickly and the brown murky water was tanking downstream. Foolishly I allowed thoughts of the Marchioness disaster to pop up in the back of my mind as the river swirled around us, then had to work hard to get rid of them.

Ably assisted by Nicky Worsley and Joanne Salley
in the Great River Race 2005

As we approached the mooring, we realised that there wasn't anyone around to take our lines and there was a distinct possibility that we could be swept past. Jo and Nicky were rowing and trying to steer alongside a huge barge, but struggling in the strong tide. With a crash and the sound of splintering wood we hit the front of the barge almost sideways on and I had to shove my back and shoulders under the side, bracing against the rowing boat to try and take some pressure off. The water swirled around and for a few terrifying minutes we thought we might get sucked between the barge and the high wall of the quay. I remember thinking that I really didn't want to end up in the horrible, murky water, and although we realised we'd narrowly avoided a disaster, we were well and truly stuck.

Eventually some Dutch rowers noticed our predicament and came to help. Once our boat was alongside (rather than half under) the barge, we were able to take a breather, but unfortunately the low tide meant we had to wait for four long, cold hours before the crane could lift the boat off. In the meantime Lin managed put her foot through a rotten section of the deck, injuring her leg, and the hatch crashed shut on her head, nearly knocking her out. Our injury count was going up rapidly and we weren't even moving!

To cap it all, the harbour master decided to moor up next to us, and succeeded in crushing the fragile borrowed boat and damaging it down both sides. For a scary few seconds, we thought that it was all over as the huge steel hull bore down on us, propelled by the tide. Jo and Nicky took the safe option and leapt up onto the side, while Lin and I instinctively rushed to fend off - as if it would actually make any difference at all! Amazingly, we managed not to swear at the harbour master, but couldn't believe how stupid he had been. We were so very lucky that no one was injured and that the boat was still just about in one piece.

Somewhat bruised and battered we eventually got home in the early hours, wondering exactly how hard this challenge was going to be if a single day had brought so many events and problems to contend with. Had we bitten off more than we could chew? A bigger bite of our elephant than we could manage? Yet when we thought about it, we had coped with it all – stress, injury, cold, exhaustion and sometimes just not knowing what the right answer was or what to do next. With those thoughts buzzing around, we slept well that night!

A few weeks later we organised a land-based fundraiser – a collection at Twickenham during the England v Samoa rugby match. It was a freezing cold day for our band of merry collectors and we hit the hallowed halls with enthusiasm. We soon found that the crowd were incredibly generous before the match and even more so in the on-site bars afterwards! I sold my England hat for £10 while Lin sold a grope for £20! Don't worry; it sounds far more risqué than it actually was as she was wearing about 16 layers in the cold, so the poor chap only really got a handful of fleece! But he went away happy and it was a fun day, raising over £2,000; you'd have laughed to see us struggling to lift the rucksack full of coins into the back of the car!

With our team, freezing at Twickenham!

Training was now firmly on the agenda as we apparently needed to turn ourselves into ocean going experts before the race. We decided to get the mandatory courses out of the way as soon as we could in case we got stuck for time later on. As it turned out it was the right decision.

April 2006 found us staying in a rented cottage in Devon with daily classroom lessons at the race organisers HQ. It was intense. In just 5 days we had to pass the RYA's Shorebased Ocean Yachtmaster qualification – we'd been told it takes most people around 5 months. Amongst other things, the course covered most of the navigational stuff we needed to know – but we even had to learn to use a sextant and calculate our position using the relevant tables. It's incredibly confusing with allowances needed for time zones, noon not actually being at noon (it can be up to 15 minutes either side), figures being made up out of numbers that all carry over at different values (360 degrees, 60 minutes and a decimal) and someone in Lithuania sneezing at the wrong time (only joking!). Even Lin with her mathematical genius head struggled; so I had no chance!

We were the only two girls on the course and the other guys were all military or ex-military and initially did seem sceptical of our ability. We've experienced this many times before in dragon boat racing and generally find that beating them head to head is the way to go in order to generate some respect! We couldn't do that here, but by the third day our hard work was paying off and they were coming to us to ask for help! We got on with the guys really well and by the time we finished, were all firm friends.

Figuring out how to use a Sextant

Every day we worked through the lessons, then headed back to the cottage for dinner and 3 hours homework before a nightcap to help us sleep. With figures spinning around our heads as we slept, we struggled to get enough rest and were dreading the exam on the final day although we did both pass the exam.

The day after the Yachtmaster course finished, we had our Sea First Aid course. As Lin and I were already first aiders, we questioned the need to do a specific qualification. Not for long though – it soon became apparent that the main difference is you can't dial 999 out at sea and there are no nice paramedics waiting to come and take the casualty off your hands. You're on your own out there and the reality is that injury is highly likely, rather than a vague possibility, so you need to be prepared. It was a stark reminder that we had a huge responsibility to ourselves and to each other to stay as safe as possible and not put the other person in a situation where they had to care for you.

The course was fun though, and was our first meeting with the lovely Jordan-White brothers, Joe and Andrew, who were also entered in our race – although I think we scared them a bit! Lin did a good impression of an injured person too, with a very realistic scream when the instructor tried to move her 'broken' legs!

Boosted and motivated by the success of passing our most difficult qualification, we planned out the rest of the year. We had quarterly meetings with Breast Cancer Care to keep track of progress, and many fundraising events. We produced a leaflet telling people what we were doing, exhibition panels for when we were out and about, and a mailing to send out to likely companies.

We gathered information about potential sponsors, asked, begged and pleaded for cash and useful equipment, courted publicity – and even got our kit off for a photo shoot for Chat magazine!! Not a day that I like to remember in too much detail – but at least it was warm! We earned £25 from the article too, so sadly it's actually true that Lin and I will get our kit off for £12.50 each!

Naked Rowing!

We learnt a lot in a short time and developed our ability to ask for help very quickly. We decided to work on the basis of 'if you don't ask; you don't get', but initially it was really hard and we were worried about rejection. The very first person that I asked to sponsor me for the Great River Race said 'no' and I was truly crushed, scuttling back to my desk more embarrassed than a very embarrassed thing. It had taken me ages to pluck up the courage to ask and I took the answer very personally – it showed that we had to toughen up and learn to be far more detached and 'business-like'.

I guess this was a good step forward in our mental preparation and apart from the Great River Race it was one of the first things we noticed that was taking us outside our comfort zone. To help with this we booked a couple of sessions with Ned, our motivational coach. We call him a motivational coach, but we were planning to use his skills to help us prepare for far more than just the motivational side of things.

The first thing that we investigated was our true goals and what drivers were behind them. We were very conscious that lots of teams fall out and argue on the way across and we didn't want this adventure to ruin our friendship. In particular, we had learnt about the intense pressure that having a different focus caused Ben Fogle and James Cracknell. James' goal was quite clear - to win the race at all costs, while Ben really wanted to get across safely and enjoy the experience. This difference affected their attitudes, moods and actions for much of their crossing and caused unnecessary suffering and tension. We didn't want the same thing to happen to us.

Ned ran us through a few exercises to establish our true motivation – which is largely driven by our key values. When he first asked us why we were doing the race, I jokingly answered "it's because of our dysfunctional childhoods". We all laughed a lot at that one, but the reality is that it may not have been far off the mark! He'd also asked what was drawing us to the challenge, yet I definitely felt that I was being pushed towards it. Over the past few years I'd 'coincidentally' bumped into so many ocean rowers it was becoming a habit, so eventually the decision to do it myself seemed like a natural next step.

Lin and I both had significant challenges to overcome in our teenage years, through very different circumstances, but with lasting effects. I believe these experiences and the way that we had to react to them, in order to continue living normal lives, has made us into the strong minded characters that we are now. We are both incredibly determined (some would say plain stubborn!) and very typical of our shared star sign, Capricorn. We are both ambitious and competitive, though not in a confrontational way, and once we've set our targets we will doggedly pursue them until we achieve them.

When we burrowed down into the key things that make us tick, there were some definite similarities in why we wanted to do this challenge and what we wanted to get out of it. Things like 'making our families proud', 'achieving something really significant' and 'testing ourselves beyond where we think it's possible' came out for both of us. Things were looking good!

Ned also asked us to develop a metaphor around the race. By that I mean an image or series of images that sum it all up. For Lin it was focusing on the end of the journey. That exact moment when she would step off the boat and see her son Liam again, after many weeks apart.

I worked on my own 'finish' scenario too, including how it would sound, smell, feel and look. And what the first cold beer would taste like! But I also liked to picture being out at sea. I had a mental view of a cloudless blue sky and intense blue ocean, with a 360-degree horizon and no land for miles and miles around. In truth, I had no idea whether being out of sight of land would put the fear of God in me, but I sincerely hoped it wouldn't! I even tried to paint the image, but I'm not much of an artist so it didn't really work. Then one day I spotted my exact image on Roz Savage's (solo ocean rower) website. I printed it off and kept it to look at and remind myself why I was doing this crazy event.

We had another major issue to tackle too. Lin was afraid of the water and worried about how this could impact on the challenge. It might come as a surprise to hear that while she's happy being on the water, if her head was under the water, she suffered flashbacks of a childhood incident in the sea when she nearly drowned. I remember teaching her to capsize a kayak when she wanted to come on paddling trips and she knew that she needed to be able to escape from an upturned boat before risking a river paddle. I took her to a swimming pool session and with me in the water next to her, she tipped the boat over and went through the escape procedure.

It was awful. Lin did all the right things; banged on the bottom of the boat, tore off the spray deck and pushed herself out quite calmly. But then the terror took over. Shaking and in tears, she made her way to the poolside. She was fine, but had had the horrible flashbacks while upside down under the water and was inconsolable. I felt terrible too – as I had made her go through the exercise and therefore caused her to feel this way.

We asked Ned if he could help. Using Neuro Linguistic Programming (NLP) techniques, he helped Lin to scramble up her childhood memory of the near-drowning event. The outcome was that her brain became unable to remember the event in its original sequence. Instead of seaweed tangling round her legs, the Smash Potato Men were waving at her from the Ocean floor. Instead of the gurgling, rushing sound of the waves, she now had the Looney Tunes music in her ears! By disrupting the thought process, the event was no longer frightening because she couldn't remember it in the same way. It was truly amazing as I sat and watched thirty years of fear simply erased in just 30 minutes!

I meanwhile had my own concerns. Not of the water specifically, as I'm more than happy in it or on it. Since junior school, I've had plenty of opportunity to be around boats and have done lots of kayaking and canoeing on flat and white water. I've been power boating and sailing, I scuba dive and surf (poorly!). And there lay the problem. I'm a teensy bit scared of big breaking waves! Which I felt could possibly be a bit of a problem mid-Atlantic. I think it's mostly because I've been trashed so often when trying to surf in my kayak or with my beautiful girly patterned Malibu board! There's little fun to be had when your kayak goes vertical, tips over backwards and slams you into the wave, especially when you're in quite shallow water and end up doing a fair old impression of an ostrich with its head in the sand as you're dragged backwards towards the beach. Equally, I've gone head over heels a few times when I've got the balance wrong on my surfboard and it's not a pleasant experience! Or maybe I've just watched the Poseidon Adventure a few too many times.

I was also worried about my reaction to fear. That might sound silly, but if you think about it, there are very few instances in our lives when we have to face absolute and total fear. I've had a few scares in my time, but when I really thought about them I knew that I hadn't been REALLY terrified for a long time and had no idea about how I might cope with the situation. That worried me a lot.

Ned tried a different approach for this. Standing on a tiled floor he asked me to think about a time that I had been truly scared. Casting my mind back, I remembered riding a horse round the fields when I was about 17. A dog jumped out of the hedge, barking at my somewhat un-trusty steed! She didn't hesitate and simply turned round and legged it! Normally if a horse bolts, the safest place to be is on the horse because if it is just messing about, it won't endanger itself, so hanging on is by far the best option. On a terrified horse, that's a different prospect. Frightened horses will run as their instinct dictates, with no regard for themselves other than to get away from the cause of the fear. It's like they are blind and deaf – any connection that you had with them is gone and they don't even know you're there. In that case, it's a tough decision whether staying on or falling off is best.

As she galloped, I lost my stirrups and experienced as I was, could not stop the horse. She was heading towards a dangerous main road – all I could think was 'I'm still here' as we thundered along, out of control. As I struggled to balance, I ran through the options and thought about letting go and falling, but knew that would really hurt – I'd tried it before!

As I clung on to the saddle, I realised that if I could just stay there, and steer the horse round the edge of the field, she would eventually get tired and run out of steam. Then I stood a chance of regaining control. Trying every trick I knew to slow her down, we tanked along, but sure enough I started to feel a change. Her pace was slowing and she was breathing harder. Bit by bit the speed and distance told and the panicked mare simply couldn't keep going. About 2 miles after the dog had appeared we came to a shaky stop.

As I recalled the story, my body language changed. My shoulders went up, I was tense and my voice was higher pitched. For every stage of the tale, Ned asked me to step forward to a new floor tile. He asked me questions about my 'state' during each minute part of the event. Eventually it clicked. My initial reaction was that although I was petrified, I coped with it and dealt with it. But, by analysing the different sections, it became apparent that I had to be in a particular state of mind in order to be able to cope, consider my options and act on them.

As I stepped forward onto new tiles, my body language transformed. My shoulders relaxed, my voice calmed and my breathing changed. I felt empowered. If I found myself truly terrified, the prompt was 'I'm still hanging in here' and then I knew would be able to deal with the situation. I became more confident that even if I did get scared out there, all I had to do was push myself into this particular 'state' and then I would become rational and able to make decisions based on what was really happening. I must admit, it felt pretty good!

Out riding on a far less scary horse with my friend Claire!

We also took time to discuss other potential issues and worked on the basis that honesty would be our best policy. I had some concerns around the fact that I'm not a particularly strong rower. Although I'm a decent paddler, height is a big advantage in rowing and a lack of height is something I really can't change. Lin being a good six inches taller and already technically strong and physically powerful was by far a better rower. I worried that I would let her down if I wasn't able to row as fast or as far as her in each shift.

In contrast, Lin suffers from moods and was worried that her down days would impact on me. When it happens, she normally just wants to be left alone and doesn't want to talk to anyone – but there's not much space for this sort of luxury onboard a 24-foot boat.

Lin reassured me that although I may not be as good a rower as she was, that wasn't going to be an issue. She knew without question that I would put in the same effort that she did. Success in ocean rowing isn't just down to rowing ability either, and Lin felt that my resilience and strength of mind would more than make up for any lack of rowing aptitude.

Likewise I was sure that I would be able to give Lin space and quiet from time to time, when her moods dictated it. We knew even then that we work so well together as a team that we should be able to manage our relationship and achieve our goals together.

Chapter 7

The next big task was to decide what to do about getting a boat, so we considered the different options available:

- Buying a kit and building it from scratch.
- Buying a second hand boat and adapting it to meet the new rules and our requirements.
- Buying a bare hull and kitting out.
- Having the boat built and kitted out for us.

Straight away, options 1 and 4 were discounted. We imagined going to sea in a boat we had built ourselves and decided it didn't bear thinking about – we knew our limitations! We simply didn't have the time or expertise to take on a project like that. Neither did we have the money or a generous sponsor to finance option 4.

So we started trawling through the lists of boats for sale to get an idea of what was available. Having spent some time onboard a prototype vessel during the Great River Race, we weren't that enamoured with the layout. We visited other boats, but none really appealed. We even asked Debra about buying her boat, Troika, and would dearly have loved to row in her, but didn't have enough money to buy her at the right time. We examined boats for sale on the main websites and discussed their previous performance and the value of the equipment that was offered with them.

Eventually, we stumbled across a boat called Atlantic 4. Formerly known as Queensgate, she held the record for a 4 man crossing of 36 days 59 minutes and had performed well in the 2005 race as Atlantic 4, before being approved as a pairs boat for the 2007 race. She was a sister boat to All Relative who was by far the fleet princess of the 2005 race. Both boats had been built by Justin Adkin who then rowed across in All Relative – a good indication to us that he had great confidence in his own work! Priced at £25,000, Atlantic 4 was technically out of our budget, but she was advertised with plenty of equipment and when we totted it all up, we thought we could meet it. So we phoned up and arranged a visit.

We first met 'Stella' on a dreary August day in 2006 on Kemble Airfield in Gloucestershire, where she was dwarfed by the nearby aeroplanes. Paul had come with us and was distinctly

Rachel Q Smith

unimpressed! But as soon as we clambered onboard, we knew she was the one and our love affair started. George (Dr Laser Beam) Simpson and David Martin, two of the guys who owned her didn't really have to do much to sell her to us – we already knew that it felt right and this was the boat for us. Ned, our coach had also come along; his former life as an engineer meant that he could help and advise us with electrical issues and other technical stuff – which was mostly over our heads at that stage.

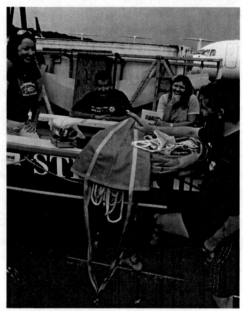

Meeting Stella – with David Martin and
Dr George Simpson (Dr Laser Beam).

Over a beer, we arranged a sea trial of the boat later that month in Hamble near Southampton and on a sunny Saturday, we joined all four members of Atlantic 4 and got the boat out on the water. George and Glynn came out for a row with us and as it was quite choppy and windy, we stayed within Southampton Water and the Hamble River. Once we'd got used to the special flexible Braca oars, Lin and I got the boat gliding along nicely and as the waves picked up, she came alive and bounced around cheerfully, despite the ballast we'd put in her central hatch. It was a done deal then as far as we were concerned – now we just had to convince the team that we could meet the price.

Our first row in Stella!

We knew that two Royal Marines, Ben & Orlando[1] were also interested in her and this fact alone discouraged us from chancing a haggle! We were so desperate to get this boat we shook hands on the asking price, with absolutely no idea how we were going to find the money! Luckily the guys understood that it might take some time and allowed us a few months to pay instalments, although I know they wondered at times if we'd ever pay up. They weren't alone!

It's a deal – celebrating the sale with former owners Neil, David and Glynn

We plodded on with our preparations and some days were better than others. We found that there were numerous people

1 Orlando Rogers was tragically killed in a plane crash in May 2011 at the age of 26; he was an inspiring and amazing example of someone who really did live life to the full.

who were keen to get involved but who inevitably let us down by not sticking to their promises or not delivering. Eventually we got pretty good at guessing who those people would be, but at first it caused endless stress, frustration and extra work. It generally was easier to do things yourself because then you knew it would get done and get done right. We had to learn to handle the resentment that built up and not to take these let down's personally, especially if it could have affected long-standing relationships. But it was extremely hard sometimes.

October 2006 brought some light relief though and we headed back to Devon for the final two of our four mandatory courses to qualify for the race entry. We met up with our instructor George at Plain Sailing in Brixham and started a fun and informative day learning what to do (or what not to do) if you ever had to take to your life raft. The afternoon was spent in a pool where we tried out getting in and out of a real raft – a big test for Lin and her fear of the water as it involved being well and truly in and under the water.

But it all went rather well and while some others actually did lose the plot and became panic stricken, Lin kept her cool, even during the mock 'storm' when we had water kicked over us and a cold hosepipe sprayed in our faces. It was fun, but made us think about how tough if would be if you had to do it in the Ocean, in darkness and with a storm raging. We didn't dwell on those thoughts for too long, just hoped and prayed we would never have to use our new found skills.

On our way back to Brixham town centre for fish and chips, we spotted George and invited him for a beer to say thank you for such a great day. A lively discussion ensued and we were invited to attend their 'Try a Boat' weekend the following May, with our boat displayed on the water if we had managed to pay for her by then!

The next day was our VHF course and this one actually proved to be a bit trickier than we first expected. It was interesting, but our instructor appeared to be the most incredibly sexist chap on the planet! Initially, we brushed off the repeated derogatory comments about girls, and his references to chatting on the phone and breaking our nails. But when he distributed the sheet with the 'Mayday' procedure on it things took a strange turn. He told us to pin the sheet next to our mirrors in our pink and fluffy bedrooms so that we could learn it while we did our hair and make up. He might have been trying to be funny, but he didn't say anything similar to the 6 boys on the same course, who were left gasping in horror at his poorly chosen words.

Our hackles were up, and by the afternoon we just wanted the day to be over. The other delegates were all very uncomfortable with the situation and had commented on it to us. Lin was livid, and it was clear that the instructor wasn't going to get anything out of her that day. I just glared at him in disbelief, knowing that with such a low impression of us, he obviously didn't rate our chances out at sea. So, I decided to remember him and his rotten attitude and use him as a motivator. He had no right to make assumptions about our ability or the type of people we were and I fully intended to prove him wrong.

That November, we had our biggest fundraiser to date. We'd been introduced to Accelerate, a Midlands based supply chain initiative, by Wayne Murcott and they'd adopted us as their 10th anniversary Charity. We'd already done one event with them and raised £3,500, but expected to generate another £10,000 at their annual awards dinner.

Held at the ICC in Birmingham and with a glamorous Oscars theme for over 600 attendees, it was by far our most important night to date. We had the boat delivered to the venue for us and we pushed her into position before helping the organisers to get the room ready. We were terrified, but incredibly excited, especially as we got to meet one of our favourite movie stars – Chitty Chitty Bang Bang! With only 20 minutes spare to get to the hotel, get changed and back to the centre, we only just made it in time to greet the arriving guests.

The host for the evening was Quentin Willson, who seemed to take a rather paternal interest in our safety. We gave him one of our leaflets, and another for Richard Hammond (our favourite hamster!) who was recovering from his high speed driving accident. We really hoped it was passed on to him, but sadly he never got in touch!

It was a fantastic night. The raffle raised a huge amount for us, and we auctioned off two signed England rugby shirts for a scary amount of cash, before a very generous chap offered to make a donation to round up the funds to the big fat £10,000 target. We were just blown away by the generosity of the guests.

Chitty Chitty Bang Bang!

Now we just had 12 months to go. At Christmas there was a little time to stop and think and I realised that the next year, our Christmas celebrations would be very different. I really felt for my family as I sat with them, eating a wonderful turkey dinner and talking about the challenge. Then as we crossed into 2007, both Lin and I realised with a jolt that time was moving on incredibly quickly and we still had no idea whether we would be ready in time. Every day we spent every single spare moment planning and working on the row. That meant a lot of sacrifices.

We trained whenever we could, having built up the length of time we could manage on the rowing machines in one session. We also found out that we needed to teach ourselves that stopping regularly to take a drink was not only really important, but it was fine to do. We had to stop being quite so competitive with ourselves and focus on the physical requirements for this particular event. We worked out that if we were doing a rowing shift onboard and needed to stop in the middle for a drink or to go to the toilet, it would not only be sensible, but essential to listen to our bodies. But it was a new way of thinking compared to our normal 'work through it' attitude and it took time to get used to.

I started getting up early to get in half an hour of training on the rowing machine before work. There was little chance to at night – as soon as I got in from work I was on the computer, writing newsletters, working on the website, updating records, planning the next event, plus a million other jobs. We just laughed about the lack of sleep and joked that it was good preparation for the race! Adrenaline normally carried us through, but we were aware that we were running right on the limit of exhaustion most of the time.

Our 15 minutes of fame was further boosted by an appearance on the TV show Ready, Steady, Cook. Hosted by Ainsley Hariott, I was paired off with Nick Nairn and Lin with Tony Tobin. It was a fun day and we enjoyed getting our hair and make up done, even managing to convince the BBC to let us wear our Breast Cancer Care t-shirts on screen. Nerve wracking though it was we laughed a lot through the filming. Although it's recorded, the show is shot in one take, with Ainsley flitting from one side to the other as the chefs do their thing.

We are often asked what we cooked and the honest answer is very little... but Nick and Tony did us proud with some amazing dishes conjured up from our chosen ingredients. It didn't really matter which of us won – we'd already planned that the £100 would go straight to the charity and the bottle of Champagne was coming with us onboard the boat for our arrival celebrations in Antigua!

With Nick Nairn, Anisley Harriott and Tony Tobin
on Ready, Steady, Cook!

We decided that we should do a test row for 24 hours without stopping, to find out what would happen! So at 10am on Good Friday 2007 we transformed Lin's house into our 'boat' for the day and started rowing. We recorded everything about the experience that we could, such as our calorie intake, how we felt emotionally and physically, and any other observations that might help our preparations. We only allowed ourselves to do things that we would do on the boat, so watching TV was out, but listening to music was OK and we used baby wipes to stay fresh, or fresh-ish! We found that not being able to shower after getting hot and sweaty was quite depressing, especially when Lin's son Liam pointed out that we smelled a bit – although we didn't notice it too much.

We ate our dehydrated expedition foods and tried a variety of snacks as well as testing our drinking regime. We slept on the sofa in our sleeping bags, but drew the line at peeing in a bucket and chucking it outside as we thought the neighbours might object! It was tempting though – as they had a barbeque that afternoon and we were tormented by the sight and smell of burgers and beer as they kept walking past the window! Later on, Liam did offer to throw a few buckets of water over us for an authentic touch, but we wimped out of that one!

We rowed on into the night and found that we really went off sweet snacks, instead craving savoury tastes, which really surprised us. Not being used to staying up all night we were exhausted, and found that although we slept, it was that weird half-sleep where you still have an awareness of what's going on around you. Lin dozed off while rowing at one point and as the night wore on, we did start to develop some noticeable aches and pains.

But we were determined not to give up and as the first streaks of dawn appeared, we knew we could do it. Despite the pain, mostly in our knees, and the pretty bad bottom sores that had developed early on, we stuck to it. We had started off the challenge with a one-hour shift each, to warm up, and so finished with one hour too. I was the last to go and it was good to know that painful though it was, I could definitely manage the 60 minutes. Lin counted down the last couple of minutes and at 10am, we called time, I stopped rowing and we gave each other a big, slightly tearful hug.

We'd done it – rowed non-stop for 24 hours in shifts and effectively spent a day onboard the boat! We learnt a huge amount from the experience, and knew without doubt that we could actually keep going for 24 hours. We'd covered over 150 miles but knew that rowing on the machine was much more intense than on the water, where we would expect to row around 35 miles a day. We'd learnt that our bottoms very quickly rubbed raw in a way we had never expected, that we could cope with examining each others sores if needed (the less said the better here!), and that we could manage on much less sleep than we were used to! We felt like we'd really achieved something big – and the hot bubble bath and roast dinner afterwards was just the best ever reward for our efforts!

Lin rowing through the night.

We constantly reminded ourselves of our goal of stepping off together as best friends in Antigua and kept this picture in our minds as we continued working all hours, as well as our normal full time jobs, to achieve what we'd set out to do. We tried absolutely everything we could to raise the funds and generate publicity for Breast Cancer Care – TV, radio and other media interviews, running a fun day, public speaking engagements, a farewell party on a boat, four days at a motorway service station, attending regattas, summer fetes and other events and generally courting publicity and asking or begging for support (and money!) wherever we went.

We sold 'memberships' and different levels of sponsorship so there was something for everyone, and we tried hard to ensure that all of our sponsors felt they got value for money. It's important to remember that when people give you money, they're buying a piece of you – they want to enjoy your adventure vicariously and without getting their feet wet. We were pleased to see that our approach and delivery seemed to work.

Chapter 8

By March, the Atlantic 4 guys were starting to put us under some pressure to pay up the balance of the money we owed – and they had a valid point. But we had a cash flow problem. Although we had a sponsor lined up to put £10,000 towards our boat, the money wasn't due in for a few weeks. We'd always thought we might end up having to take out a loan to cover the last few costs, but only ever imagined it would need to be at the last minute. So we had a tough decision to make, but we took a chance and decided to borrow the money, with the aim of paying it off as soon as we could.

At last, the boat was ours, and Lin collected her on the first weekend in May to take her down to Brixham in Devon for the Try a Boat weekend. Driving our smart, new, liveried SsangYong 4x4, which we were loaned for 2 years, she drew lots of interest driving down the motorway. I guess driving a car with pink stripes down the side and names plastered all over it, while towing a weird looking boat will attract some attention. Sometimes it even generated sponsorship when we stopped for fuel! Paul and I joined Lin later that evening and we slept (or tried to sleep) in the cars that night because the boat was full of expensive kit that we didn't want to leave unsecured.

We got her onto the water the next morning for the event and Lin and I slept onboard together that night. It was unbelievably exciting to lie there, bobbing around in the harbour in OUR boat! We felt like kids on a camping trip for the first time, and as we gazed up at the stars, we wondered how it would feel in the middle of the ocean.

We used the weekend to start stripping the old sponsors' stickers off the boat and convinced a whole new group of supporters that they really did want to sponsor us! We made some firm friends that weekend, friends who supported us right through the challenge and who are still friends now. It was a really special few days.

But as with all good things, it had to come to an end. Lin took the boat back to her new home at MDL's Hamble Point Marina and we compared notes on a rather severe dose of land sickness! It's something we've both had before, but this time lasted for a couple of days – making working at a desk quite unpleasant as our computer screens swirled and swayed in front of our eyes. Neither of us really suffers badly from seasickness and it's only happened to us a couple of times, but land sickness can make you feel just as bad!

Lin making herself at home!

Time was starting to pass at an alarming rate and we still had a lot of work to do on the boat. I arranged for her to go to LDV (the van manufacturer) in Birmingham for a beautiful coat of bright pink paint, which we saw for the first time at Women's Henley. We were so proud of our little pink boat, although the Atlantic 4 boys were mortified and called up the first owners, from when she was called Queensgate, to share their horror at seeing 'their' boat painted girly pink!

With so much still left to do, I was starting to get really concerned. But we sat down and listed all the jobs to do, then took the plunge and booked our flights and hotel for La Gomera. We had reached the point of no return and whatever happened, we were going to be on that start line on 2nd December.

The summer was both fun and frustrating, but most of all it was incredibly hard work. We both put in a huge amount of effort, but it cost so much, financially, in time and emotionally as we lived, breathed and dreamed our challenge. I spent every spare weekend working on the boat and drew some comfort from the feeling of bonding with her while I drilled, fixed, wired and cleaned. As I sat in the little cabin on dry land, I peeked out and wondered how it would feel to see waves towering over the boat, maybe crashing across the deck. Although it was good to consider how it would make me feel, I quickly pushed any negatives aside with my very positive mental picture of the finish.

We were also still finding that relying on others to step up to the mark and deliver on promises often ended in more work for us, as we were frequently let down in one way or another. Someone once asked what the biggest lesson was that I learnt from the challenge and disappointingly, that was probably it. Yet we didn't want to jeopardise long-standing relationships that were genuinely important to us, by having pointless diva strops! So we ploughed on regardless, but became even more sceptical of offers of help.

I spent a weekend at Lin's house scrubbing the mattresses from the boat, which were a bit yukkie after 4 boys had spent 49 days onboard, and sanding down the oars and rudder which Lin then painted. In the summer of 2007, there was one Friday when massive flooding covered much of the Midlands. We were due to meet up for a collection in Swindon the next day, but it took Lin 4 hours to do a 2-hour journey in horrendous conditions and I narrowly avoided spending the night in the car on the M5 motorway. Eventually I realised that there was no way I was going to get to Mayfield Park where we were supposed to be camping, so gave up, turned around and went home. We had to cancel the collection.

Eventually I joined Lin on the Sunday when the water had subsided a bit, and we started applying our sponsors' stickers onto the little pink boat – and she looked beautiful. We performed a 'De-Naming' ceremony complete with Pimms toast to Neptune and then moved the boat to Ned's home in Gloucestershire for a while so that he was able to work on the electrics and some other jobs. I squeezed in a much needed week away with Paul in Greece, which helped to smooth over some of his worries about 'the pigging row' as he'd taken to calling it. Then I spent the next few weekends at Ned's helping make the changes needed to bring the boat up to the required standard for the race.

This work took me well out of my comfort zone, not least because there seems to be something fundamentally wrong with the idea of drilling holes in boats! Especially when the boat in question is soon to be your life support in the middle of the Atlantic! I was also a stranger to the art of using power tools and my experience of electrics pretty much limited to changing a light bulb, so I learnt a huge amount during those days, and had no idea just how valuable this knowledge was to become just a few months later. This provided our first introduction to Sikkaflex, the most sticky, gooey substance known to man (or rower). We used it to fix and seal all manner of things on the boat, normally with a good helping getting smeared all over ourselves in the process. Ned and I coined the phrase 'just Sikkaflex it', on the basis that if something needed fixing, Sikkaflex would do the job!

Even with Ned supervising, drilling holes in boats is just plain wrong!

It was good to spend some time with Ned too and an incredible boost to see that his confidence in our ability to complete the whole challenge never wavered. He'd made a huge contribution to our challenge both in time and financially and it meant a lot to know that he really believed we could do it.

In between we spent four days collecting at Roadchef's Strensham Services on the M5. The team there were incredibly helpful in accommodating us at a time when most of the area was still under flood water and we had a great reception from literally thousands of people who stopped by to chat. It was a highly successful event – but one incident left a nasty memory for us.

On our second day, we were approached by a lady who had seen our exhibition panels inside the building. We were always very honest in detailing the terms of our collection and how the money was used and split between us and Breast Cancer Care; but she seemed to have taken exception to our approach.

She came over to tell us how disgusted she was about the cost of taking part in the race. She thought we should abandon our entry and work purely to raise money for Breast Cancer Care. We were shocked and speechless, as it seemed to us that she didn't really have a grasp of the concept of sponsorship – where you volunteer to do something and people pay you for it. All sponsored events incur a cost, and we counterbalanced ours by trying to raise an exceptional amount for the charity.

The lady ranted on and accused us of being 'two rowers out for a jolly', and at this point we had to laugh. Anyone who thinks rowing the Atlantic is a jolly is clearly barking mad and as we pointed out, we'd had to learn to row specifically to take part in the race! That did take the wind out of her sails a bit, but we clearly weren't going to change her mind. She went away muttering about what a disgrace we were.

We stood in silence for about half an hour – which is most unusual! Both of us were mulling over her unkind words; words that had instantly put such terrible doubt in our minds. Was she right? Were we really such terribly selfish people? Were we doing a bad thing after all? Should we call a halt to it all right there and then? Gingerly we broke the silence and started to run through it, swiftly coming to the conclusion that she was wrong. We had to believe in what we were doing – Breast Cancer Care believed in us, as did hundreds of others. Hers was just one opinion, and while she had every right to express it, we had an equal right to disagree.

I name this rowing boat… Barbara Ivy

We held an official naming ceremony for Barbara Ivy at the Cotswold Water Park, attended by friends and family. We named the boat after two inspirational women who sadly lost their battles with breast cancer - Barbara was Lin's mother in law and Ivy was my grandmother. My Mum, being the most religious person we know, blessed the boat for us in an emotional speech and sprayed champagne over the bows to seal the deal with Neptune.

A couple of weeks later, we were ready for our sea trials. Due to the problems with handling this kind of rowing boat in coastal water, we had researched a good place to spend the required 48 hours onboard, without causing too much of a problem for ourselves, or hopefully for the emergency services. Much as we admire Lifeboat men, we really didn't want to have to get rescued by them!

So, we headed off to Poole Harbour on the first weekend in September and finally got on the water at 6pm on the Friday, after a lengthy interview with the very lovable Jake Kavanagh, then features editor from Practical Boat Owner (PBO). Jake had been enthralled with our challenge from early on and put together a three page feature in the magazine – fully understanding the needs of our sponsors and helping to get them valuable coverage too. He still claims to dine out on our story!

We went for a short row that night and decided to stay moored up for safety. The next morning we phoned the Coastguard to explain what we were doing – just in case anyone reported a freaky pink boat with two mad women doing odd things onboard! We planned our route round the harbour, allowing time to stop and run through a series of exercises every so often. We plotted our position on the chart every couple of hours and practiced using the anchor and sea anchor, the GPS and radio, and even tried out the AIS system – which happily pointed out that there were a number of large ferries in the area.

It wasn't calm that day, which was probably good experience, and the frequent wash from passing boats had us bouncing around all over the place, even though we'd taken the precaution of adding ballast. Keeping out of their way was a challenge in itself as a little pink rowing boat is an unusual sight in Poole Harbour and we created a lot of interest. The most terrifying though were the ferries, especially the Condor catamaran, an evil looking vessel if ever there was one. We kept well clear of them!

We anchored up on the west side of Brownsea Island and donning our sexy (!) fluorescent orange survival suits, had a go at getting in and out of the water. This proved a bit tricky with a fully inflated life jacket, but it was good fun, even though we disagreed on how useful these suits would be. My thoughts were that they are fine for inside a life raft, but having an open neck, would not work very effectively in the water – as they would eventually fill up! So we talked it through and agreed to disagree while I tasked myself with finding a kind sponsor who would buy two proper immersion suits for us. The deal being that if we got them free, Lin would agree to take them instead of the orange suits. Needless to say, we were soon the owners of two Musto dry suits, fit for the worst the ocean could throw at us.

48 hours in Poole Harbour

We had great fun eavesdropping on the radio calls from other boats on Channel 16 and picked up some good tips for how not to make calls! That night we settled down to sleep after an evening spent learning knots and chowing down on our expedition food. The only thing that woke us was when the tide went out leaving us grounded on the sandy bottom at a bit of an angle! Next morning though, nature overtook the proceedings and although we'd hidden our luxury Luggable Loo in the front cabin to spare any blushes, our top halves still stuck out of the hatch when we were 'sat upon'! So you can imagine the looks from nearby boats as we called a cheery 'good morning' to them!

That day we rowed pretty solidly round the rest of the harbour until we stopped to meet up with a photographer (from PBO) in the late afternoon. It was an exhausting two hour shoot which involved us rowing like billy-o up and down against a strong tide, while the photographer tried to make some waves for us – but we got some fabulous shots. Then we headed back to Cobbs Quay to take the boat off the water, but made the fatal mistake of cutting the corner of a marked channel – perhaps more easily done than you'd think when you're travelling backwards! As we felt the boat get heavier, we pulled harder, only to find we were stuck fast in the mud. Although I should point out that this was an area that we had rowed over 3 times before without incident – that's our excuse!

As the tide rapidly receded, we tried to push off with the oars and Lin hopped over the side into the stinky gunge to try and push us free. Tiny fish started to flap in the puddles of water and the seagulls pottered towards us in a slightly scary, stalker-like manner! But stuck we were and there was nothing for it other than to wait for the tide to come back in and refloat us.

In good ocean rowing style, Lin put the kettle on to make a coffee and some apple and custard, so we could enjoy a snack while waiting for the tide and waving at passing boats. I meanwhile tied some tools to myself and hung out of the stern hatch to detach the rudder, which meant that we would float free more quickly. As we got going again about 30 minutes later, the boats that passed us couldn't believe we'd freed up so quickly, but we were just hoping that no one sent photos to the newspapers, that would have been too embarrassing to bear!!

Meanwhile the fundraising continued to go well and our sponsors seemed happy with our delivery. Some were so impressed with the exposure they were getting that they even contacted us to donate more items! By now we'd reached a stage where we would just ask for whatever we needed. Lin became known as the 'blagging Queen' and we prided ourselves on being confident enough now to ask for anything – we'd come a long way!

One final session with Ned focused on pain management, which was something we were quite nervous about. We certainly expected to feel some pain out at sea and had come to terms with the fact that it would happen. Blisters in particular seemed unavoidable, and we were worried because they are disproportionately painful and debilitating when you think about what they actually are. Ned of course challenged us and suggested that the best pain management was to avoid the injury. At first we thought that was a ridiculous idea because all rowers got blisters and we were bound to as well.

But we talked it through and realised that in sourcing our special gloves, agreeing to stick with plain wooden oar handles and having been given Blister Sticks to rub on sore patches, we might be able to avoid or at least reduce, the pesky blighters in the first place. Maybe we did have more control than we thought and should not simply accept that getting blisters was inevitable.

We moved on to an exercise where Ned had us both hold an ice-cube in the palm of our hands. He joined in too and the task was to think about the feeling of pain. At first it was funny, but within a few seconds, it did become very painful.

Our hands stung and burned as the cold seeped through our skin, and we tried out the different techniques to cope with it. Analysing it was one option – what did it feel like, what colour or shape could you associate with it, did it change or move? For a while I pretended that I was friends with it and invited it to stay, then showed it the door! But I found the most effective solution for me was to accept it and then ignore it. The pain from the ice got to a certain point but was bearable. It certainly hurt, but it stopped getting any worse and I was coping with it and able to contain it. After a couple of minutes Ned suggested that we put the ice down, but by then we were completely absorbed by the exercise. We agreed that we needed to beat the ice, so quite perversely, sat with dripping, cold and stinging hands until it melted completely. Maybe that was a demonstration of the weird kind of mentality that would make the difference between success and failure for us.

One of our final events before we left the UK was to host a fundraising party for all of our supporters. But we were so busy by then that we had to find a willing victim to take on the majority of the work for us. We decided on a nautical theme and hired a Thames River boat courtesy of Crown River Cruises – Bobby the owner is also an ocean rower! Music was donated by a DJ and a singer who were both friends of Lin, while Jo and Lou drew the short straw and kindly volunteered to make all the other arrangements.

Despite the huge logistical effort it took to get the event off the ground, everyone had an amazing night and it was great to look around the boat and see so many of our generous supporters who had made the trip to London to attend. Many of those who couldn't get there had donated prizes for the raffle, which generated another healthy boost for the bank account. Jo and Lou had done a great job and it was a fitting send off before the next stage of the adventure.

Long days continued in the last couple of months and we were under a huge amount of pressure from work, family and the row. Even after the tough weekend packing the boat (imagine squashing an elephant or two into a Mini!) ready for shipping, the break we'd hoped for didn't materialise and we were both still living, eating and sleeping the challenge. We simply couldn't wait for the day we set off for La Gomera, or better still, the day we started rowing, leaving all the real life hassles behind.

Just some of the food and equipment we had to pack into the boat.

Chapter 9

Monday 16th November was an early start as I had to fly from Manchester to Gatwick to meet up with Lin and also Elin and Herdip from Dream Maker, another women's pair in the race. Paul took me to the airport and it was a difficult time. Our last weekend together had been really nice but awful at the same time and at one point he'd actually asked me not to go, which I was furious about.

I understood his concern to a degree and knew that he'd been having horrible nightmares for months. Dreams where I was in trouble at sea and he couldn't do anything to help – and I felt terribly guilty about it. But I also resented it as I had never once said 'don't go' when he went away with the Royal Marines. I felt I had always supported him to the hilt while he was putting me under seemingly immense pressure and it felt like I wasn't getting that same level of support in return. It was a really difficult time and I didn't know what to do about it.

By the time I got to Gatwick I was feeling a bit ropey and curled up for a snooze while I waited for Lin. Once she arrived we sat looking out over the airfield and both had a tearful moment. The guilt of what we were putting our families and partners through was very hard to bear, but we also knew that we couldn't let it affect our decisions. We'd come too far now.

By the time Elin and Herdip arrived, we were back on good form and had a good old girly gossip together. Arriving in Tenerife, we literally sprinted from the airport and only just made the last ferry by standing on the ramp so they couldn't close it, while one of the girls bought the tickets. We arrived in La Gomera in darkness, though it was warm after the dismal British autumn, and were met by some of the other rowers who took us to see the boats. Our beautiful Barbara Ivy was already there, sitting on her cradle, high up on the wall at the entrance to the harbour – we thought she looked like a little princess! Happily, she seemed to have travelled well and we couldn't see any major bumps or scrapes, so we said goodnight to her and headed off to our hotel.

By 10pm we were both in bed, utterly exhausted, when Dr George 'Laser Beam' Simpson sent a text to our satellite phone from the UK to check that the love of his life, Barbara Ivy, was OK and to berate us for letting the side down by staying in instead of partying. One text read....

> ☒ *Get down to the Blue Marlin right now. You're ocean rowers, not a pair of nuns!*

We ignored him! We had a lazy first day and slept in late for the first time in months before exploring the lovely town of San Sebastian and checking the boat over in daylight. She seemed to be enjoying herself in the sun, lording it over all the other boat minions around her!

We stood on the black sand beach and gazed out to the horizon, thinking about how it would feel when we rowed off into the distance, when there would be no turning back. It was quite exciting to think about, but it also sent a slight chill down our spines – the horizon seemed an awful long way off and we had no idea what was beyond it. There and then we promised that when we got to the other side and stepped onto land, we'd do it together, holding hands, as the best friends we were now. We knew the crossing would test our relationship to the limit, but we were determined to not only make it in one piece, but remain as close as we'd ever been.

Gazing across the black sand beach to the horizon!

Just in time, we made it into shelter (aka the nearest bar!) as the heavens opened and San Sebastian was drenched with torrential rain and strong squally winds – what was going on? We hadn't ordered weather like this and we didn't fancy being out

77

on the water in it! Gradually more rowers and the race organisers turned up and as we clearly weren't going to get chance to work on the boat, we settled for a beer instead!

The next 10 days passed in a blur of activity, although we both felt strangely calm and at peace with ourselves. We worked on the boat every day, making final fittings and adjustments ready for scrutineering. Eventually we were ready and spent over 3 hours going through the boat and kit with Tony Humphreys, the race Scrutineer and Duty Officer. He seemed impressed with our level of organisation, and when he left we had a relatively small list of jobs to complete before he'd give us the final go ahead.

Disappointingly though, we were missing one vital piece of kit. I had organised the loan of a life raft from Avon Inflatables and we had both run through the requirements. Avon confirmed they could supply a raft to meet the regulations and duly sent one to us. The race organisers confirmed we had the right paperwork, so assuming everything was OK, we'd simply packed it onto the boat and sent it off.

However, the valise case clearly showed that we were missing a 'Solas B' kit, which is a pack of items that would help you stay alive in the raft if you were stuck there for longer than 24 hours – something that's a distinct possibility on the Ocean. I felt awful and was wracked with guilt as I should have spotted this sooner. How on earth were we going to find the pack, or make up the equivalent contents on such a tiny island with very limited shops? I could tell Lin was mad, and I was kicking myself for the oversight, but she kindly didn't take it out on me and simply focused her energy into helping track down the missing bits.

Bizarrely, I had actually packed some of the more unusual items we needed, just because they were lying around and looked interesting – even if I had mistakenly thought the portable radar deflector was some kind of inflatable fender! Hey, until you've seen one, no laughing! Still, luckily there it was, along with a few other things that we duly ticked off the list.

The funniest thing we had to do was track down a set of leak stoppers, which are normally conical wooden bungs to plug leaks in the life raft. Bearing in mind that most Gomerans don't speak much English, trying to explain what we needed was hysterical! We started by trying to draw pictures and act out the scene of a raft puncturing, air hissing out and stuffing a bung back into the hole. It's amazing that we weren't arrested for making obscene hand gestures! Eventually, we found a chandlery with a catalogue and were able to point out just what we wanted. Amazingly the leak stoppers did arrive 'mañana' just as the man promised, so we must have been doing something right.

We spent two days sanding down the hull of the boat and applying a new coat of antifoul paint. It's designed to prevent stuff like barnacles growing on the bottom of the boat as they slow you down. Antifoul is pretty noxious stuff and we got covered in it. But the white colour we'd picked mixed with the red that had been used previously and we ended up with a lovely pale pink to compliment the bright pink above the water line! The final job was applying reflective tape around the water line and we even added dots of it along the gunwales for a true 'bling' effect.

The downside was that all the bending underneath the boat had caused Lin to strain her foot. She was in a bit of pain and contemplated going to the hospital to get it checked, but it did ease so she didn't go in the end. We had no idea then that it was to become a real problem and were just glad that it didn't seem too serious… how wrong you can be.

We started to get more messages on the satellite phone too:

☒ *Mandy Howlett: I'll be thinking of you both every day, Take care and I love you both. Go Pink, go naked, GO GIRLS! Xxx*

☒ *Paul: Mornin! Get up woman and start making that boat the safest, fastest thing on 2 oars! Have fun in the sun!*

We normally worked right through the heat of the day to get our jobs done in time, but did treat ourselves to a couple of siestas! Although we were busy, our organised approach in the UK made life a lot easier in La Gomera and we didn't have the same panic as some other crews. It also meant that we could enjoy a few nights out, including a rower's fancy dress party when we went out dressed as a 'pair of tits'. Dr George's Mum makes knitted hats and had made us one each, shaped and coloured like boobs in honour of our charity! We wore the same dress from our sponsor Joules and had a fun evening with the other loons in the Blue Marlin!

It was great to meet up with all the other rowers too – many of whom we already knew from the UK, and we look back on the time in La Gomera with happy memories. Even so, the approaching challenge was clearly playing on all the rowers' minds, and it's surprising that the Blue Marlin never ran out of beer as ocean rowers have a tradition of 'drinking every beer like it's your last!' Because it may well be!

With Orlando Rogers and our 'boob hats'

Just before we all left, Manolo, the owner of the Blue Marlin, cleared a section of wall for us all to write our names on, just as past rowers had done. Somehow seeing our names up there made it all the more real.

Pam, our helming friend from South Africa had sent over the very same friendship bracelet that we'd made for her 10 years before in Hong Kong as a symbol of good luck. We fixed it inside the boat where we could both see it, together with two 4-yen pieces, sent to us for good luck by a school class in Japan. Pam also sent us a message:

⊠ *Wishing you both strength in body & mind, calm seas & wind behind you. You will be in my thoughts until safely across. Love Pam.*

I never actually believed that I would die, even on the very worst days at sea, but when you're waiting for the start all sorts of thoughts cross your mind. There's also the terrible guilt of what you are doing to your loved ones, combined with the feeling of inherent selfishness (not really something to be proud of) that's required in order to succeed in a challenge like this. Although you have to be positive, you must also be realistic about the risk you are taking, and the voracious partying reflected the mood.

Leaving our little bit of history on the wall in the Blue Marlin

We particularly got on well with Joe and Andrew (Jaydubyoo), Elin and Herdip (Dream Maker), Bill and Pete (Gquma), Ben and Orlando (Go Commando) and Nick and Jon (No Fear). But to be honest, most teams were friendly and it was easy to strike up a conversation with any of them. We also had chance to get to know the crews of the two support yachts, Sara of Douglas and Kilcullen.

We were surprised to find that not all teams quite as friendly though. Naturally some kept themselves to themselves, but we really struggled to find common ground with the two girls from another female pair. We didn't like their attitude, and were appalled when they told us that they planned to mislead the organisers about the amount of food they were taking. They felt that 90 days food was far too much and as they expected to finish in 65 days, they were going light on the rations. In our mind, that was cheating and we found it hard to accept.

There's always been criticism of the high entry fees for the organised races, but now being in a position of experience, I'd say they are worth every penny as being part of a race provides 24/7 support on and off the water. In addition to the back up of the Duty Officer, the support yachts are out on the water with you, sailing short-handed, with just 3 crew members, to ensure there is room on board in case they have to pick up a rowing crew or two! They have to carry extra food and medical supplies, as well as provisioning for themselves for up to 3 months at sea as they go backwards and forwards around the fleet. The crews were lovely too and on hand to help with all sorts of questions and queries. We both felt so much better knowing that they were going to be out there.

We had a quiet last night with family and friends, opting for pizza at a restaurant across the road from the hotel. Our friends Tim and Fi had travelled to La Gomera to see us off, along with my Mum, my brother Gordon and Dave. Paul had arrived the day before and we snuck away early to spend some time alone together. I was so pleased that he'd come to La Gomera, and when he saw for himself just how organised and prepared we were, compared to the other competitors, I think it did help him to come to terms with what we were doing. It was important that after the stressful final weekend at home we had some great memories and as he hugged me and told me how proud he was, I knew that everything between us was going to be fine.

The last supper! Paul, Fiona, Tim, Mum, Gordon, Dave

Race day was surreal. Early in the morning, I had my last bath for however long it was going to be and as I lay there in the warm water, I tried to absorb the memory because I knew I'd miss it very soon. I felt very calm but detached as we had breakfast and managed to keep a lid on my emotions as Mum handed over Christmas and birthday presents, while Gordon and Dave presented us with the essential companion for any rowing boat – a ship's bear they'd named Sebastian, after San Sebastian our departure port.

We walked to the boat with the last few things to go onboard and busied ourselves with the final few jobs, but were constantly interrupted for photographs and hugs. It was a strange feeling. I did feel a bit sick, but as you'll know from the dragon boat racing days, that's pretty normal for me. We both really just wanted to get going; to row away and leave the craziness behind. It was a beautiful sunny day with a gentle breeze in the right direction, and I tried not to think too much about what was over the horizon, or what the future held.

Gradually, everyone moved away to take up vantage points around the harbour. As each rowing team made their way to the start, cheers went up and it was a very emotional time. Everyone had put in such a massive effort just to make it to the start line and now we all had the same immense task ahead. I'm not particularly religious, yet I said a quick prayer that we would all make it safely across.

Heading to the start line.

Paul stayed with us right to the end to cast us off the pontoon and eventually, the time had come. To cheers of our own, we slipped the lines and pushed off onto the water. Slowly, we rowed out into the bay towards the start line. It was really noisy with loads of boats on the water to watch, all sounding horns and shouting encouragement. I turned round to Lin and we just grinned at each other, hardly daring to believe that we'd achieved so much and had actually made it to the start line. The years of hard work had paid off and now we could forget them and focus on the next part of our incredible journey.

Noon drew close and we held back a bit; we didn't feel any need to be jostling for position with the other boats when there were 3,000 miles to go. At last the start horn sounded and a huge cheer went up from the crowds on the water and on land. We grinned at each other again and decided that as that was the start, perhaps we should start rowing! We were off!

Chapter 10

The sun was shining and the sky was bright blue and cloudless as we rowed away from La Gomera on water that glistened and sparkled. There were boats everywhere, and we shouted our encouragement to other teams. Supporter's yachts and the organiser's speedboat with Amanda onboard buzzed around us and it seemed strange to shout our goodbyes, hoping that the next time we saw her we would all be safely in Antigua.

Our plan was to row for 6 hours together, then stop for an hour and eat together before taking out the stern rowing position and switching to our two hours on, two hours off shifts. It felt so good to be out on the water as the noise gradually melted away, leaving just us, the ocean and Barbara Ivy. Alone at last! We stopped regularly to drink and after a couple of hours agreed that we should attempt to get the water maker running.

The water maker was the one piece of kit that we hadn't been able to test properly before setting off. We'd serviced it but you can't run it in shallow harbour water because you're likely to suck up a load of silt and clog the filters. We had taken it out and stripped it down, then replaced the coarse filter in La Gomera, but we still had to get it running in situ. Without the water maker, it's race over because it's your single most important item onboard. It was therefore inevitable that as soon as I switched it on… it didn't work!

I scrabbled around in the greasy, stinking hatch, starting to feel slightly queasy while trying to follow pipes round and make sure they were all attached properly. We knew that you had to pump the system first to get it running, and that a particular valve had to be open, but all that seemed to happen was that we ran a leak and water started to collect in the hatch. Lin started to show signs of getting frustrated at my incompetence although to be fair, neither of us could actually remember exactly what we were supposed to do.

I climbed inside the cabin to get the instruction manual, and instantly felt worse. We had talked about taking sea sickness medicine, but opted to go hard core and allow our bodies to adjust naturally – knowing this meant we were likely to get sick for a while, but hoping it would be fleeting. As I tried to work my way through the manual, waves of nausea washed over me and after one more session fiddling round in the hatch, I had my head over the side of the boat. Lin hates seeing or hearing others who are ill because it makes her feel sick too, so I felt like I was really letting her down.

First day on the oars… before seasickness struck!

I called Dr George on the sat phone for instructions and bless him, though he's never let us forget the early call for help (and tells everyone we were distraught and in tears – which of course we weren't!), he went through as much as he could remember. We swapped over and Lin's frustration deepened as she started to feel queasy too. Eventually we heard the reassuring 'tock tock' noise as the pump started and water began to trickle out of the right place. The sense of relief was immense, although we knew this was just one little hurdle to overcome.

⊠ *Debra Searle: The 1ˢᵗ week is probably the hardest.*
Takes time to settle into the routine & to get over
any sea sickness. So be gentle with yourselves. Big
seagoing hugs.

As we carried on rowing we felt much better although not quite up to eating anything more than tinned fruit in syrup, which is a great cure for seasickness (the glucose in the syrup helps maintain your energy levels and the fruit travels fairly well in either direction…!), when we stopped after our 6 hours. Dusk was drawing in and the waves stilled. We sat and gazed out at the view, barely able to take it all in, as we listened to the water lapping against the sides of the boat. Suddenly, we heard a puffing, swooshing noise close by and realised with great excitement that the dolphins had come to pay us a visit!

I think we had about 15 of them swimming around and under the boat for half an hour or so, checking us out from all sides. We were ecstatic to see them, especially on our first day at sea, and it really did feel like a confirmation that what we were doing was OK. It felt as though the dolphins had come to wish us well and look after us.

The euphoria didn't last long though, and as the dolphins left and the last of the sun disappeared below the horizon, the wind whipped up ferociously. We were still in what's known as the 'acceleration zone'; a section of water around the Canaries that channels the wind and it can be quite dangerous. The waves grew and grew, and in the darkness, I was struggling to keep the boat stern-on to them. After about 30 minutes of battling, I admitted defeat and we decided together that we should put out the sea anchor while we were still feeling below par. We reminded ourselves that we had promised our families to be safe, and that this was just the first night of many. It wasn't a time to try and be heroic.

We deployed the sea-anchor without too much difficulty and breathed a sigh of relief as the boat turned her nose into the wind. The lights made La Gomera and the next island, El Hierro, seem very close and we monitored our drift with an intensity verging on obsession. We could see and hear the big ferries right through the night, together with some of our fellow competitors on their VHF radios. We even got chance to radio Pete Collett for a chat, one of the solo rowers who happened to be nearby and apparently that was his last radio chat with anyone until he got to Antigua. Luckily he wasn't so near that he could hear us throwing up, even when we performed a perfectly synchronised chunder – simultaneously over port and starboard! Even we laughed at that one throughout a pretty uncomfortable first night.

⊠ *George Simpson: Hi there ladies, good first night?*
Hope the seasickness isn't so bad. Row South, South,
South, South, South, South. Gxx

The next morning (Mon 3rd December) we hauled in the anchor and happily accounted for all components - result! Although we both still felt a bit queasy if we sat up inside the cabin, rowing or sleeping was fine and we stuck to our 2 hour shifts for the next 24 hours, all the time heading south. The waves seemed huge at about 10-15 feet and there was a strong Easterly wind howling around. But the boat just bobbed along happily and we quickly got used to the massive swells, even enjoying the feeling of being picked up and pushed along. I concentrated hard to keep the boat lined up properly and to take advantage of surfing when I could, enjoying the feeling as the boat did exactly what she's built to do.

Dolphins thrilled us again with another dusk visit, getting amazingly close to the boat. It was tough rowing that night in the strong wind, with land still seeming so much closer than it really was. We named El Hierro the never-ending island as it just didn't seem to get any further away! At first light we rested and let the boat drift along. We were making good progress in the rough conditions – although to be quite honest we weren't entirely sure what constituted 'rough' at this point!

With great excitement, we started to get a few more text messages when we turned the sat phone on at noon for the required 1-hour. We decided to keep a record for the future and started to write down all of the messages in one of the notebooks. We also had our first visit from one of the support yachts, Kilcullen, which we spotted on the horizon as they sailed over to say hello, then later on, as we were both feeling much better and able to eat, we decided to do another all nighter.

☓ *Duty Officer Tony: Wind forecast to remain same direction and force for next few days. Many boats report steering probs, advise drogue use if necessary. Be safe.*

Over the next few days the conditions didn't change much. Our advice from the wonderful Tony, our Duty Officer at race HQ was *'if the wind/waves take you in the right direction – then ROW!'* So we did. But it was incredibly tough and once or twice in the early hours we put the sea anchor out again because we couldn't see what was coming our way in the dark and it seemed too dangerous for one person to be out there alone. The waves had doubled in size and we reminded ourselves to be safe, wearing our harnesses and staying clipped on all the time. We also experimented with a drogue, but Barbara Ivy persistently swung round to go broadside to the wind and waves, leaving us less confident than when we were fully in control and steering.

When we heard about the man overboard incident on Titanic Challenge on the first night and the team deciding to retire, our hearts went out to them. But it reminded us about what was important – and staying attached to the boat was a high priority and man overboard was a mistake that we were planning to avoid. In all honesty, we had thought the Titanic Challenge team preparation was somewhat lacking in La Gomera and I have to say that I'd never go to sea in any boat with Titanic in the name; nonetheless it must have been a terrifying experience for them.

⊠ *Jo and Lou: Fish Joke #1. Who robs banks & squirts ink? Billy the Squid! Keep it up, we are impressed, you two are just amazing.*

This was to be the first of many fish jokes!

We had our first 'ship drama' on day 5 when we saw lights in the distance. We radioed several times and switched on the Sea-Me, but got no response. It was a big ship, and we watched as it passed by some distance away with no harm done. For the rest of that day there was little rowing done. The wind and waves created two distinct patterns, neither of which was good for us. Lin volunteered to stick her head out the back and we played around with drogues again for a while, but with no luck, so exhausted, we eventually gave up and went to bed.

Our hands were bearing up well with the combination of our kangaroo skin golf gloves (from Kakadu) and blister stick treatment. Even so, I had developed a particularly persistent blister buddy who I named Bertie and mentioned in the blog, then got a bit worried when Bertie started to receive more text messages than I did!

By day 6 we were just about getting into the swing of things when we were surprised by a visit from support yacht Sara. Blimey, Stu and Andrea were so early that morning they very nearly caught us without our clothes on! They told us that Atlantic Jack and Jaydubyoo had both damaged their rudders in the stormy weather and had to make repairs. We felt really bad for both teams having such bad luck so early on and thanked our lucky stars that our rudder seemed to be holding up; although we had noticed the steering line was rubbing on a scupper cover and needed to be monitored. Steering was proving to be problematic at the best of times, with the wind and waves at loggerheads and a boat determined to swing broadside at the first opportunity.

A visit from support yacht Sara of Douglas

Life onboard brought many other challenges and the constant movement was one of the biggest. The boat pitched and rolled continually and the monitor we had in the cabin to measure tilt simply swung wildly from one extreme to the other most of the time. The extreme motion made doing even simple things ten times harder than on land – so putting on a t-shirt or brushing your hair became a major effort. All too often you'd let go of one of your essential 'three points of contact' and find yourself flying across the cabin at speed, before progress was abruptly halted by impact with the GPS or something equally as painful!

Out on deck, standing and walking was nigh on impossible, although we tried to stand and do some exercises to stretch our calf muscles as often as we could. Movement was pretty much limited to stepping into or out of the cabin. It was around 2-3 metres from the cabin to the rowing seat and the journey from one to the other usually took place quickly and while keeping your centre of gravity as low as possible.

We were also starting to become aware of potential problems onboard. As we hadn't actually seen much of the sun in the first week, our batteries seemed to be running a bit low, so we changed course slightly to try and catch a few more rays on the bigger rear solar panel during the daylight hours. We headed more towards the west, rather than south west, which meant that the wind was side on, but we were able to ride the waves a bit better and the charge seemed to improve a little.

⊠ *Paul: Hey ho girls – well the weather here is crap – work is depressing – the house is cold (forgot to turn heating on) and a pigeon pooed on me. How's your weekend?*

We were now well and truly in the shipping lanes and keeping a slightly anxious watch. That night we saw what seemed to be a fishing boat getting nearer and nearer – there was a big spotlight at the back so we thought they might all be working on the nets rather than having anyone on look out. It got very close and there was still no reply on the radio, so I ended up hopping around outside in just a jacket and knickers, while trying to work out what the etiquette is for letting off a white collision flare! I mean, how close should you let them get before you fire it up?

Eventually the fishing boat moved away and Lin was straight back to bed while I sat outside and nervously waited until it was safely out of sight. Two more massive tankers passed us the next day too, steaming along at 18 knots and only 2 miles away from us, according to the AIS. We could see the huge bow waves clearly, but hadn't heard or felt anything as they snuck up on us. No noise from the engines, nor vibrations through the water. It was scary stuff and I certainly seemed to be more bothered by the ships than Lin was.

Even by now we were both getting fed up of being constantly wet and cold, and our bottoms were starting to show signs of some nasty sores forming. I'd taken some cheap waterproof trousers onboard but found the pocket holes opened the wrong way round and sometimes let a cheeky wave in. So, I took to wearing them back to front so the pocket flap faced the right way. I certainly wouldn't have won any awards for style, but looking back, I think those trousers saved me a lot of problems later on and certainly helped keep me drier and warmer in those early nights.

Chapter 11

Problems, problems and more problems were looming. On day 8 we tested the connection for the flexible solar panel that we'd brought to boost our power supply, before fixing the panel onto the boat. We plugged it in and saw the charge to the batteries decrease straight away. This told us that we (or I!) must have wired up the connector wrongly – thankfully Lin knew enough about electrics to work it out, as I didn't have a clue. But that meant I had the fiddly job of unscrewing and rewiring it and I got the distinct feeling Lin was less than impressed with my electrical knowledge, or lack of knowledge. Although I was sure that I had wired it as per the instructions the first time, I accepted that I must have got it wrong and cracked on to fix it.

    ⊠ *Paul: Hi again – just taken a look at action photos of Barbara Ivy on web site – there's no one rowing! Your progress though is good and steady... so steady as she goes.*

When I plugged in the rewired flexible solar panel, hey presto, it worked! But it was still too rough to open the rear hatch and secure the panel on the side of the cabin – waves were breaking over the stern on a regular basis and we didn't want to get our only dry-ish haven of the cabin wet if we could possibly avoid it. Still we had a bit of excitement in the form of a huge pod of dolphins whizzing by in the morning. They must have been feeding and it was a fleeting sight, but there were loads of them, all jumping clear out of the water in complete synchronisation over and over again. It reminded me of just how special it was to be out there and able to witness things like that.

The next day was a fraction calmer as the wind changed direction and helped to push us further South West. We kept rowing overnight again although we were both quite tired and Lin had started reporting that she was sometimes falling asleep while rowing. Around the same time I often thought I could very faintly hear African music and singing at night. Being so far from the coast it was highly unlikely and probably just the first sign of madness setting in! But hallucinations or not, somehow it made the dark nights a bit more bearable and reminded me how lucky

I was to be out on the water. It all sounded very funny but we did need to concentrate hard at night, as there were still big ships around, often getting pretty close. We couldn't wait to get out of the busy stretch and lose some of that worry.

By day 10 (Thursday 11th December) we were tired and definitely starting to feel the strain of our constant battle against the huge swells and strong winds. It just wasn't what we had expected on a daily basis. It perhaps sounds like we were naïve, but that's not the case. We never thought it would be easy and we expected some sizable rollers in stormy weather, but not every single day with no relief. The small number of texts received that day only emphasised our low mood and there was a distinct lack of high jinks onboard. As we were now so low on power, there wasn't any spare electricity to make water for washing, and feeling a little on the unwashed side is pretty demoralising and did nothing to help us feel better, so we just tried to laugh and joked about how well our dreadlocks were coming along!

⊠ *Roger & Amanda: Remember when stuff breaks duct tape is like the force, it has a dark side, a light side, and it holds the universe together!*

Conditions were becoming so rough that we abandoned actually rowing for sitting outside on the seat and just steering. Rowing in those conditions usually meant one oar buried and the other one not even touching the water, with the boat jiggling around like a Weeble – remember them? 'Weebles wobble but they don't fall down!' Bruised shins generally followed as the oar handles regularly connected, leading to giraffe like patterns up and down our legs. Just steering made for a more comfortable ride for the person resting and actually felt like we made better progress. Sally had suggested it, and it did seem to work although I too fell asleep in one session – following Lin's example!

The big waves were often interspersed with little waves that speeded in from the East like torpedoes. We called them sidewinders or whizzers and they slapped into Barbara Ivy sideways on, spraying and soaking us in the process. She would then leap and bounce around like a stung horse and do her very best 'Weeble' impression! It was pretty horrible, especially at night when you could hear them coming but couldn't see them – you just felt them hit!

Day 11 was a bit sunnier, and a little calmer and at last we managed to get the solar panel fixed onto the boat. It gave our power an instant boost and meant that we were able to run the water maker for a while. We'd actually resorted to hand pumping water with our emergency water maker the day before. It was still cold at night though and we bundled on the layers – even wearing our woolly 'boob hats' for rowing in the dark.

Rough and windy conditions from day one.

⊠ *Dave Evans: Howdy paddlers. Brrrrr serious frost this morning. Finance Christmas party tonight – oh joy! Paddle hard, you're just about there.*

We felt a bit more rested after the night of steering and surfing, and there seemed to be fewer ships around now which proved far less stressful. With time to look around, I was finding the changing sea constantly fascinating and that day we went across a large patch of weird, squally water when the surface suddenly went all gnarly and choppy for a while, then cleared up as quickly as it started. Very strange!

We also kept thinking that we could see fish jumping, but couldn't be absolutely sure and decided it could just be hallucinations! We were both being proper girls about the little splashy waves coming over the side, but they were quite cold and caused a few squeaks as they hit the boat and got us!

Unlucky for some, the 13th December (even though it wasn't a Friday) was a particularly bad day for us. Overnight we noticed the reading on our electrics going down and down, until they disappeared altogether, meaning that our batteries were deader than road kill. We wondered if the electrician who fitted our tracking beacon in La Gomera had buggered something up. It was a serious problem as no power means no water and no navigation – which is pretty much game over. Many calls to Duty Officer Tony and Dr George later, we figured out that because we'd left the flexible solar panel plugged in overnight it had reversed the flow and effectively drained the batteries.

We were distraught to find out that it was our fault that it had happened, but simply hadn't known any different. It left us with no choice other than running on zero power through the night and the next day, although luckily we only saw one ship, which was far enough away not to be a concern. But having no power at all for a while was quite a worry and we felt very vulnerable.

Eventually we got hold of Ned too, but to be honest we found it more frustrating than anything. Ned, being his normal calm self, kept saying reassuring things like 'maybe we could run resistance on the panel' or 'start switching things off to see how much charge the water maker is drawing'. Despite his good intentions we were already pretty stressed and just got more wound up as we already had everything switched off and didn't understand what things like 'running resistance' meant. Ned is an expert in his field, and has endless patience – but our impatience came from our realisation that unless you are out there it's impossible to appreciate just how difficult it is to do anything onboard the boat. Even simple jobs take 10 times longer than they should and dealing with the boats' constant movement was a bit like trying balance on a bucking bronco or the wobbling floor in a fairground 'crazy house'.

So through the day we had to move the huge, heavy life raft twice, open the hatch underneath and check the charge going into and out of the batteries in order to isolate the problem. To our surprise and delight during this weightlifting challenge, we found a tiny stow away crab crouched behind it, looking more than a little terrified as we messed up his living arrangements. We called him Cyril!

⊠ *Hilary Williams: Mileage creeping up. Great stuff. Glorious day but Christmas shopping Chester – crammed! Wish I was there. Hil x.*

Sadly Cyril didn't hang around for too long and decamped through the scupper back to the ocean as we continued trying to find a solution. Typically it was the sunniest day yet, but things weren't looking good. Having no power opens up a whole load of possibilities – not all of which had outcomes that we wanted. Top of our list of fears was being forced to retire from the race, get picked up and have to sink the boat (so she wasn't a danger to other shipping), or being run over by a ship that couldn't see us. We felt gutted and tearful, and unsure of what the future of our race was going to be if we couldn't fix the problem. We knew that we didn't want to give up but simply didn't have the answers we needed.

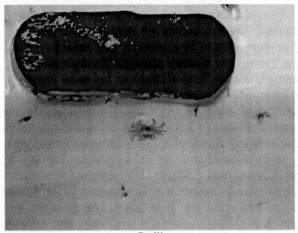

Cyril!

Earlier, George had joked on the phone that 'you don't need electrics anyway' and the more we thought about it individually, the more we both realised it was true. Sure it would be much harder if we hand pumped water to drink, more dangerous without proper lights at night and would probably take us a lot longer. But we felt it could be done – after all, we had battery powered spares for most of our essential equipment such as the GPS and with our Capricorn stubbornness, we had to at least give it a go before admitting defeat.

Lin came out of the cabin to take over rowing and in one glance, we both knew exactly what the other had been thinking. We simply couldn't contemplate losing our beautiful Barbara Ivy and were prepared to push ourselves to new limits to save her… and our race. Our problems were far from over, but we agreed to give it a go and instantly felt stronger and more able to cope.

We cheered up after a good night rowing, when the wind and waves died down to leave a beautiful clear, calm night which allowed us to marvel at the stars above. It was hard work without any power, as we had to rely on head torches to see the compass and watch while we were rowing. We also had to keep an even sharper eye out for ships so that we could react in plenty of time. But we adapted well and I actually found it easier to switch my head torch off and literally follow the stars to navigate.

The next day we had lots of phone calls, emails and texts with Tony and Ned as we tried to figure out a solution to the power problems. After a series of even more tests (and moving the 36kg life raft yet again!), we ended up rewiring the circuit board to bypass the regulator. The regulator is the gismo that's supposed to control the flow of power to the batteries, rather than stopping it entirely. By excluding the regulator from the circuit, it meant that the solar panels would charge direct to the batteries – although this would bring a new problem as we would then run the risk of the batteries 'over-cooking'. The solution then was to check the battery charge several times a day and control it if it got too high. So we gave up on moving the life raft and lashed it to the centre of the deck over the runners in the stern rowing position.

   ⊠ *Bill & Hilary Jordan White: Joe & Andrew send*
    their best wishes that you fix your electrics. All the
    very best, Bill & Hilary JW.

Rewiring was a difficult process to manage as the screws on the circuit board were really tiny and the boat was getting thrown around quite a lot. We both needed to be in the cabin to do it, with Lin reading out the instructions, Tony and Ned on standby near their phones, and me doing the practical stuff. It was pretty terrifying and we were desperate for it to go right as my shaking hand hovered close to all the important looking soldered stuff on the circuit board. One wrong move could have been a disaster. Luckily Ned had the foresight to prepare wiring diagrams, which meant that it was clear which wires had to be undone and fastened together and there were no unexpected slips of the hand. We hoped and prayed that we'd done it right. Later on we discovered that we weren't the only ones with power failure as a number of other boats had similar problems.

With the power sorted, we were able to enjoy a stunning day at last, with relatively calm seas, clear blue sky and hot sunshine. We really wanted to see a bit more wildlife as we hadn't had any visits for a while, apart from Cyril the stowaway crab and Fearne & Reggie the Storm Petrels who seemed to be following us.

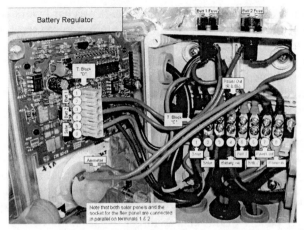

The row-saving, spaghetti-like wiring plan that Ned had prepared!

⊠ *Ned Skelton: Great to see your tracking beacon working and your position looks good. I wish you sunny skies. Hugs, Ned.*

With just 10 days until Christmas, we spent another night without power as we switched everything off again and nursed our sick batteries back to health. It was a huge relief to find they held a charge overnight and we were able to run the water maker for a short time the next day. We also noticed that again we only received a handful of text messages, before we worked out that it was probably because it was the weekend - we really missed the 'bored workers' getting in touch!

That night was particularly eerie without any artificial light and we both had a sense of 'something' around the boat. We didn't actually see much more than a few flashes of phosphorescence as things chased other things around in the water, but you never know what's there in the depths…! We definitely saw and heard some fish jumping, but apart from that the water was unusually still and the wind had dropped which made it quieter and more spooky than normal.

We tried to write a blog every day and both enjoyed sharing our ideas and deciding together what to write. Some days it was tricky as there wasn't much to say other than rowed, ate, slept, but we knew it was important for our supporters to live this experience with us stroke by stroke. We were also excitedly planning a special treat for Christmas Day, our very own '12 Days of Christmas – Ocean Edition'.

By day 15 (Sunday 16th December), the batteries were showing enough promise to run the water maker for a whole 1.5 hours. We cheered up noticeably at the thought we might be in luck and able to make enough water to treat ourselves to a hair wash on Christmas day!

Settling into life onboard – Lin preparing dinner!

As we got used to rationing our power, we named ourselves 'stealth boat' and joked about sneaking across the ocean without anyone noticing. In fact, Tony told us that the girls onboard Atlantic Jack had tried to radio us two nights before when they were only 3nm away from us. When we didn't answer, they phoned him to say they were worried about us! It was nice to hear they were concerned, but he pointed out that as we had no electrics, we wouldn't have the radio switched on unless we really needed it – we weren't really ignoring them!

> ☒ *Jo McKelvey: Lou & I went to France – although the purpose was to buy vats of red wine & though we didn't actually row the ferry, we still felt we were sharing your experience. J&L.*

Day 15 was also the day we both got to row NAKED for the first time! Until then it really hadn't been warm enough and we were starting to feel a bit misled by all the stories we'd heard about all over tans from other rowers. Lin called the Jaydubyoo boys for our regular catch up and not only were they doing fine, they were also naked! It was very funny and a little odd to think about the fleet of little boats bobbing around the Atlantic with all those naked people in them!

Warmer though it was, the rowing was still hard, as the wind and waves were not helping each other or us. But by then I was coming to terms with life at sea. Not every moment was pure enjoyment, but I certainly wasn't hating it and on the whole was happy with life on the ocean.

The hard rowing continued into the night - broken only by a close encounter with a ship, which we think was called 'Sagamore'. We saw it some way off and went into action, switching all our electrics on and radioing, only to hear the Atlantic Jack girls somewhere nearby and already in contact. Unfortunately, we also heard them ask the ship to divert in order to avoid them, but right into our path! Just great! We thought they might at least have mentioned us, and the other rowers in the area, when they made contact.

Eventually we got in touch with the ship and confirmed that the Captain could actually see us. We did realise that they would get pretty close as they passed, and we stopped rowing for a few minutes. Even so, there was one point when we were drifting a bit too quickly in their direction and I suggested to Lin that she backed us down (rowed backwards!) – like that was a really smart and practical idea in the middle of the ocean! But back us down she did and although the ship passed within just a couple of hundred yards, they went on by. The encounter left us both on a bit of an adrenalin high though; that ship was huge!

With Atlantic Jack in the vicinity, Tony had sent us a few texts with position information to find out whether we were planning a coffee morning together! It's really unusual to see another rowing boat once you've left La Gomera, so you can imagine our surprise the next morning when we actually spotted the bright orange of Atlantic Jack about half a mile away while we ate our breakfast. We waved and radioed, and were certain that the girls must have been able to see us but they ignored us and carried on South. We thought they must have been getting us back for not having had our radio on a couple of nights before, but apparently they never even knew we were there!

▣ *Philippa Campbell: WOW you've made it to sea! Cleaned oven and car today – thought about you with very different priorities. So proud of you x.*

By now we were both feeling really tired and even Lin had stopped enjoying the breakfast meals. I'd gone off them long before. The breakfasts were really rich, creamy and sweet to make up their 800 calories, but they were making us gag a bit. So we had a think about how we could adjust our food routine over the next couple of days and the Snickers bars that the Atlantic Angels gave us in La Gomera were starting to look very attractive! We started to have one a day for breakfast and I have to say that much as we love them, it took both of us some time to be able to face a Snickers again once we'd finished the row. Now I can only manage a bar if I'm doing sport and it took Lin three years to eat a whole one!

We also heard that the weather was likely to change for us in the next few days which meant that we might have to go onto sea anchor for a while. Sally and Clint sent us a message with the advice to go as far West and South as possible while conditions were good – so we set to the task and pulled hard to keep the miles ticking along while we could.

Chapter 12

Day 17 was sunnier so we both got naked again – it was such a liberating feeling! Though my urge to stretch my arms out and shout 'yee haa' at the top of my voice was soon curtailed by Lin!

Overnight we'd had another close encounter with a ship and this one was quite scary, as he got really close to have a look at us. But what concerned me most was that I really struggled to wake Lin up to help. With my anxiety about a collision, I felt we should be making more effort to contact the ship on the radio, but Lin was much more laid back and went straight back to sleep – with the instruction to wake her if it got any closer! She hates to be disturbed, and I felt really bad for waking her up again as the boat headed towards us.

It did pass by very close, but just as I thought we were out of danger, it suddenly changed direction and came straight towards us. I don't know whether the crew saw our Nav light and decided to investigate, or diverted to miss another boat. Either way, I found myself in the bizarre and unwelcome situation of seeing huge bows bearing down on us and having to turn due North and row like hell to get out of the way. It's not something I ever want to repeat. I was a bit shaken, but it took some thought to decide how to broach the subject without causing an unnecessary argument. Eventually I simply said that I thought we should be more persistent on the radio in future to avoid this kind of incident.

⊠ *Kim @ Yachtpals: Checked your progress, good job you two. Grrrl Power. Kim on a sailboat in San Francisco Bay.*

By mid morning on Day 17 the less favourable wind arrived and after I'd spent a whole session rowing with just one oar, we swapped over only to find that the increasingly strong wind meant Lin wasn't able to get the boat straight at all. Margaret and Cath onboard Atlantic Jack decided to call us up as they were stuck in the same weather system. But it seemed to us as though they really just wanted to make sure that we were stuck too and not overtaking them! We reassured them that we'd just let out the sea anchor to stop the wind and waves taking us South East faster than we could row South West!

The lack of progress was frustrating, although the hot sun meant we were able to make plenty of water and enjoy sitting out on deck. That's when 'Hawkeye Lin' spotted a large brown splodge in the water. On closer investigation the splodge stuck its head up and became recognisable as a huge turtle. He was an awesome visitor and kept us entertained for about half an hour, swimming around the boat and nibbling the stuff growing on the rudder. We named him (or her!) Treacle after the Scott Mills show on Radio 1! We got some amazing pictures of Treacle the turtle and his posse of little stripy fish friends.

Treacle the Turtle!

We had to stay on sea anchor for 36 hours in the end, which was a real bore, especially as we felt we'd both perfected our single oar and 'Eddie the Eagle' (just picture a ski-jumper on the slope!) rowing techniques; which were ideal for the choppy conditions! While we sat it out we entertained ourselves with some children's puzzle books that Mum had packed and played our favourite games – planning the things we would do and places we would go when we got home. I dreamed about spending a weekend in the Lake District or surfing in Devon, and we both enjoyed the 'lottery winner' game over and over again!

But our favourite entertainment by far was thinking about all the food and drink we were missing – which could be considered as a form of torture really. We'd start the game off with the question 'If you could eat (or drink) anything in the world right now – what would it be?' We never got bored of playing and top of the list was normally fresh, cold water, a cold beer or diet coke, fresh fruit and vegetables, a roast dinner, ice cream, pizza, Indian food, Chinese food… you get the picture!

By far the biggest bonus of this enforced rest was that our salt sore covered bottoms dried out and started healing – and then itching like mad! But the scratching was sheer bliss and we must have looked like a pair of ponies rubbing on a gatepost!

Later on that day we spoke to the Jaydubyoo boys again. They'd tried to row but ended up getting blown miles off course. So they soon gave up, put out their anchor and did some fishing instead! We kept an eye open for any changes to the conditions, but the waves continued to be big and the wind strong. It stayed sunny though and we were able to top up our water supply to a whole 10 litres! Getting a longer sleep was great too, though incredibly uncomfortable in the boiling hot cabin as the boat bucked and cavorted over the top of the waves, her nose held fast by the sea anchor.

Our supporters were sending in some wonderful text messages and I remember thinking that I wasn't unhappy at all just then, although I would rather have been rowing towards Antigua. Towards the end of the day it clouded over and as Lin went outside to boil the water for our evening meal, we had a real downpour. It was horrendous – but like a proper trooper, she put on her British stiff upper lip, stuck it out and got drenched for her thoughtfulness! Although she did consider washing her dripping wet hair at one point! What a star!

⊠ *Hilary Williams: Morning, you may have power but I don't have water – frozen pipes and overflowing loo! And still no decorations up or cards posted.*

Our second night on sea anchor was far from uneventful! We left the Nav light on, but noticed soon after dark that it had gone out. The power supply was fine for a change, so the only other option was the bulb. We dug around in our spares box and found one, but when I staggered up to the bow end and tried to change the bulb, I realised that I couldn't actually reach the light without sitting on the cabin; which was pretty impossible in those conditions. Even for Lin it proved extremely difficult as it was at the very extreme of her reach and she wasn't able to balance properly because the sore foot she'd had in La Gomera was still showing signs of injury and hampered her. As a temporary fix, we taped a torch to the AIS aerial, but knew it would only last for a couple of hours.

There was no other option now; we had to find a way to change the bulb. So Lin, being the tallest, had to stretch over the cabin in the dark to unscrew the light bulb while being thrown all over the place. Our somewhat clumsy solution was for Lin to lean over the front cabin completely off balance, while I hugged my arms around her hips and hung onto the grab rail on the cabin. It was literally face to ass as I tried to stop her sliding around and bruising too much! Unfortunately, during this exercise we lost the light cover to Neptune when it popped out of Lin's pocket and splashed into the water as we bucketed over a particularly steep wave – so we had to be innovative in finding a replacement. Ten minutes later a Tesco plastic bag was duly duct taped into place over the new light bulb and we were back in action!

By the morning conditions had eased and despite massive swells running south, we were able to row again and make steady progress South West. The swell was undoubtedly the biggest we'd seen so far, with waves probably 50 feet high and quarter of a mile apart, coming in from our starboard side like big rolling hills. It took several seconds to row up the front of each one, followed by a second or two of feeling like you were poised on top of the world with a view for miles around, before gliding gently down the back into the deep trough to meet the next mountain of water.

☒ *Philippa Campbell: Sounds like the wind is not doing you any favours – makes me think of Griff's helping hand. Hope you can feel the Helping Hands urging you on!*

After the enforced rest on sea anchor, we realised we had gathered some fish friends on our journey and saw a load of stripy buddies whenever we emptied the loo bucket! But we suspected they might be 'dun for' as a result of their chosen diet – you'd have thought they could have found a tastier lunch! We did hope our little friends wouldn't attract any bigger pals though, as we'd heard that some boats further west had reported seeing sharks. It wasn't that we were particularly scared of sharks, and I've been scuba diving with them before, but were both in agreement that we didn't feel any pressing need to see one close by.

We carried on rowing through the night and into the next day, making good progress and maintaining our course, boosted by the brilliant news that we were the only boat with zero miles of backwards drift on sea anchor. In fact our GPS had told us we drifted 1 mile South West – actually in the right direction for once!

Every other boat in the fleet had gone backwards in that period and it gave us a further thrill when we realised that our drift also meant that we had passed Atlantic Jack again!

At times it seemed like there was one thing that broke every day, and now it was the turn of the outside GPS to bite the dust. We spotted water condensing inside the screen and it suddenly started looking a bit like an Etch-a-sketch gone mad, before randomly and repeatedly turning itself on and off. Although it had been really useful and gave us something interesting to watch at night when we followed our route on the little screen, it wasn't essential and we disconnected it, knowing we'd be fine without it.

The foot well outside the main cabin continually filled up with water and we still didn't have enough power to run the electric bilge system too often. So every rowing session started with hand bailing water out scoop by scoop before venturing forth from the stuffy cabin. Our luggable loo lived in the foot well, and we laughed about sitting on it with water sloshing around our ankles. With the lid down it also doubled as a seat for whoever was boiling water for the meals. A kind of kitchen/bathroom combo area!

View from the rowing seat.

By now the moon was up every night, nearly full and very bright – making for much nicer rowing in the dark hours. Although we discovered that at those latitudes, the moon comes up like the Cheshire Cat's smile rather than the more vertical crescent we're used to. The first night I saw the orange tips come up over the horizon like a pair of horns, it looked like something was on fire and I started to understand why so many sailors are superstitious. To begin with neither of us had a clue what the strange light was on the horizon and we were a bit awestruck until we saw the whole crescent and realised it was the moon. On other nights the moon lit a silvery path across the waves for us to follow, while phosphorescence glittered and dripped off our oar blades like something from a fairy story. Sometimes a drop of phosphorescence would land inside the boat and glow for a while before fading.

We also found that Fearne and Reggie the Storm Petrels had discovered a talent for some classy night time 'bat' impressions – and seemed to take great pleasure in making us jump as they swooped by, brushing past just a wingspan away from our heads!

☒ *Dave Evans: There are 7 different species of sea turtles and the most known is the green sea turtle. It can swim up to 20 miles per hour. I say attach a line to the little fella?*

With three days left until Christmas (22nd December), the hard work on the oars continued as the sea never let up or calmed for a minute. Cloudy skies reduced our power and we noticed the Nav light dimming at night sometimes, forcing us to go back into 'stealth mode'. The full moon helped, but when it set in the early hours we were left with a horrible 'dark before dawn' part of the night. Then there was nothing. It felt like a black void with no light at all and sometimes you could sit and wonder where everyone was on the planet – you were completely and utterly alone in the dense darkness. Our hearing became highly sensitive and we tuned in to the approaching rumbles, like a freight train in the distance, warning us that a big wave was on its way. Then we simply prayed that we had the boat lined up right and waited for the inevitable soaking.

On one such night, I could feel that the waves were huge and almost dreaded daylight when I'd be able to see them. As I rowed along, they continually landed on the deck, soaking me. A slight lightening of the sky as dawn approached meant that I could make out the silhouette of the waves as they rose up around the boat. Not such a good thing as a wave shaped like a pyramid, and not much smaller, grew to a point towering over the boat, before curving, and landing square on my head. I was not impressed!

The horizon is level with Lin's right oar
– rocking boat and pitch dark nights!

⌧ *Gordon: Hi Both. Don't let the last few days get you down. You are still doing sooo well and making us all proud. Roll on 500 for champers! Love G&D.*

We were getting lots of amazing text messages on the sat phone, many from people who we didn't know, and from all over the world. It really kept morale up and our mood was further improved by a brief visit by some dolphins who darted by with barely a glance our way. We'd adjusted our food routine now we were more settled and enjoyed our Snickers bar in the morning for breakfast, then a hot meal for lunch and dinner. We snacked in between whenever we fancied it and never felt hungry although we weren't eating anywhere near the 5,000 calories a day that we needed. Back home we'd vacuum packed whole load of Mum's fruit cake, but were mystified because we couldn't find any in the first few day bags of food. Eventually we tracked it down and it became a favourite treat. The only things that we enjoyed more were chocolate, mini Cheddars, toffee popcorn, Baileys, and the treat to beat all others… tinned fruit!

We'd heard about flying fish territory from rowing and sailing friends and thought we'd seen some jumping out of the water but weren't entirely sure. Until later on that day when we found our first two tiny flying fish on the deck. Lin managed to save one, but the other was definitely a gonner! And no, we didn't eat it, it was far too small – just wouldn't have been worth the effort! But we gave him a suitable burial at sea.

Small flying fish – bigger ones were up to 8 inches long!

By now we were getting close to the 500 miles travelled mark. This was our first big distance goal of the crossing, and we had decided to celebrate our achievement by cracking open one of the many small (quarter sized) bottles of champagne that we had stashed onboard. It seemed from the messages that our supporters were really getting behind us and seemed as excited about the milestone as we were.

⊠ *Gordon: Hi both, just to let you know at 5am this morning you were on 495. Probably 500 by now so get the champers out! Well done!*

Sunday 23rd December – and we'd been at sea for three whole weeks. It seemed like a lifetime and we wondered how long you had to be out there before you could officially call yourself an Ocean rower. We decided that three weeks should just about do it and I tried out my new title proudly as I rowed along - Rachel Smith, Ocean Rower!

Amazingly we hit a personal best for Barbara Ivy of 55 miles in 24 hours. It took us over the magical 500-mile mark and the first celebratory Champagne, drunk stylishly out of our thermos flask cups, tasted wonderful! Even more wonderful was the news that the girls on Atlantic Jack were rowing hard and desperate to catch us.

Rachel and Lin – officially 'ocean rowers'!

But we did have some frustrations too. Ned unknowingly highlighted the issue for us when we received a text saying he was concerned about us because there had been a lack of news in the last couple of days. The concern was completely genuine and we realised it was shared by many of our supporters. Yet we were just so busy surviving and coping, we couldn't really understand it in our somewhat selfish little bubble world of the ocean. We were trying to row 24 hours a day, manage the power problems in cloudy conditions, cope with life onboard and keep everyone happy. We thought our position was being posted on the race organisers web site regularly, so we couldn't understand what the problem was. But we didn't know that the beacon supposedly sending our position back to the website wasn't working! If we had known, it might have helped us to put this perceived pressure from everyone at home into some sort of perspective. What it did do was prompt us to try harder with our blogs and if nothing exciting was happening onboard, that's what we told everyone. It helped to remind us about what those at home were going through and how tough it was for them too.

Due to the power problems, I hadn't used my iPod much because recharging it was a luxury use of electricity and as we often had no light, we relied on sound to warn us of any problems at night. But I decided I was going to have to give it a go as the sound of the wind whistling round the boat was driving me nuts. It endlessly whined round the aerials and howled down my ears. In contrast the wave noise didn't bother me at all and in fact I found it quite comforting, but the wind noise just tormented me. The music did help to blot it out, but it never completely ceased.

I had some audio books and podcasts on the iPod too, so spent some time giggling away to Chris Moyles' Radio 1 show, thinking about how bizarre it was to be listening to his familiar voice in the middle of the Atlantic. I'd also taken the latest Dick Francis novel as I love his horse racing orientated thrillers. This one was no exception and I was soon absorbed in the story. So absorbed in fact that I actually got really scared one night! As the hero was being attacked at a polo club, I suddenly got a sense that there was someone lurking right behind me. I risked a nervous glance over my shoulder to check, and of course there was 2,000 miles of ocean before the nearest land. But it was too late by then and my imagination was running wild. I had to switch off the audio book!

To provide some entertainment, we both used to gaze at the clouds and pick out shapes. This was normally great fun and the day we saw a proper cube shaped cloud we decided it had to be aliens visiting in a poorly disguised space ship. One night Lin saw a skull and I saw an 'eye in the sky' with the moon shining behind the clouds like an eye ball. Another night it was Santa towing an empty sleigh – probably getting ready for Christmas. Very spooky!

Big sky and endless cloud formations.

⊠ *Pam Newby: Wishing you small seas and a good tail wind for the most extraordinary birthday of all! My thoughts and love are with you both.*

The night before my birthday (which is on Christmas Eve) was massively hard for us. The waves were reasonably big as normal, but the flow seemed to be unusually fast and unrelenting. We were

Rachel Q Smith

moving incredibly quickly without even rowing and to be honest the oars caught the fast water and whipped out of our hands, bashing into our already battered shins and adding to the giraffe patch pattern of bruises! We simply couldn't stop and had to keep steering just to keep the boat upright. The moonlight helped us to see a path across the rolling waves and we spent the night hours feeling like we were on a never-ending cold and wet rollercoaster ride. We found out from the Jaydubyoo boys the next day that we'd done an unbelievable 29 miles between midnight and 6am – something of a record, as apparently we were the fastest moving boat in the fleet that night. We'd even covered more ground than the South Africans and the Royal Marines! Bring it on!

Chapter 13

☒ *Chris Bailey: Thinking of you both & following your progress. So great to see people making their dreams happen. Enjoy your Christmas.*

It was certainly a very different birthday and Christmas, but in all honesty it wasn't the best I've ever had. On Christmas Eve we decorated the boat with tinsel and tried hard to stay upbeat in what were again cold and dreary conditions. I opened presents from my family including a teeny birthday cake, complete with candle!

Happy Birthday!

On Christmas day we had hoped to spend a couple of hours drifting along in the sun, opening our presents together and phoning home, but it was clear that our idyllic day just wasn't going to be possible. It was still fun in a way as we took turns to don Santa hats and open our presents, but it just didn't get close to the picture we'd built up in our minds as we instead found ourselves battling with the wind and waves again. I did however take the opportunity to treat myself to a fresh, clean t-shirt as the one I was wearing was 3 weeks old and about ready to walk off on its own!

Everyone at home had tried so hard to make Christmas special for both of us we felt a bit guilty for feeling so miserable. We both got some lovely presents which had a lot of thought behind them – not least in making them small and light enough to carry with us! It was nice to know people were really thinking about us that day and we were inundated with messages wishing us well, supporting and encouraging us. But we did miss home, the people we love, and that special atmosphere of Christmas.

⊠ *Clint & Sally: Weather 4 week good. Waves could be rough, no nasties on horizon. Enjoy, it's the only xmas you'll have at sea. Sit back & smell the flying fish. Happy xmas!*

We'd started to notice that bizarrely whenever Lin was rowing, or even sometimes just on deck, waves would come rolling over the side and she'd get soaked. At our rowing shift handovers I would try to be helpful, give a bit of feedback on the conditions I'd experienced in the previous 2 hours, and then line up the boat so she could get going quickly. But Lin usually took a bit of time to get settled in, by which time it seemed the waves had spotted her and were already threatening a dousing. She started to mention the fact that I could go a whole session with just a few splashes, while she got drenched with stinging salt water every single time. It was really strange and we never found a good explanation for it, but I quickly learned to bolt for the cabin as soon as I got off the rowing seat so I didn't get wet too. We did joke about it, but for Lin it really wasn't funny, just tedious and uncomfortable, and on top of her still sore foot, it took away any enjoyment there was in rowing for her.

⊠ *Amanda: Merry Xmas. Hope you enjoyed your lunch… I did! Thinking of you & wishing we were sat in the bar. Can't wait for Antigua. Stay safe. P.S. You're getting loads of messages on the website. You've got a real fan club! (Soppy but hey, who cares – so proud of you keep rowing!!!).*

After putting on my new, fresh and dry, un-musty t-shirt and opening my brilliant and very innovative presents from home, I went outside to keep Lin company while she was rowing. Of course, within ten minutes of sitting there, a wave curled round the back of the boat and dumped right on my head. Literally! So much for the lovely clean and soft t-shirt; I was completely soaked from head to toe, which was not my idea of a fun start to

Christmas day. It was easy to understand why Lin was getting so fed up with it.

> ☒ *Debra Searle: Happy Christmas! Raining so hard here. Wish I was with you both. Soak it all in as you'll never have another one like it. Big Christmas hugs.*

Christmas dinner proved to be a success but took some real initiative to get it ready. We'd been determined not to miss out on our turkey, but a full roast really isn't possible on a rowing boat so we had to compromise a bit. Lin took the role of cook while I steered, and the first challenge was to open the tin of turkey. We thought that our Gerber multi-tool had a can opener on it, but it seemed not. So we resorted to a bit of impact technology, punched a hole in the tin and then hacked away round the edge until we could scrape the meat out!

> ☒ *Jo & Lou: Lin & Rachel, we wish you a very merry Christmas in your little pink boat. We'll raise a glass or 5 in your honour. We are so proud of you. A fish joke from an actual cracker: What's the fastest form of transport at sea (apart from Barbara Ivy)? A motor-pike!*

The cooking pan proved to be a bit smaller than we expected and was tricky to balance on the cooker with the peas and carrots sloshing around inside. We made gravy in a thermal mug and after some thinking, came up with the idea of mixing the Smash potato in a chocolate mousse packet – after the mousse had gone overboard of course. The chocolate mousse had been our biggest disappointment food-wise, so it wasn't like we were ever going to eat the disgusting stuff!

> ☒ *Tony: Santa sends 18-29kts Easterly winds for next 48 hours. Merry Christmas, Ho Ho Ho or is that Row Row Row!*

So Christmas dinner a la Ocean tasted wonderful, although I found it very difficult to steer and eat at the same time, with the wind blowing the food off my spoon on the short journey from bowl to mouth. Trying to eat it while it was still warm, I bolted it down far too quickly and in the rough conditions, ended up coughing some of it back up again. All in all it was an experience I'll never forget!

> ☒ *Tim & Fi: Hi girls – Happy Xmas. Hope the turkey & champers went down OK & you've managed to have a break from rowing. Stay safe xx.*

Opening Christmas presents.

Boxing Day was a little more relaxed as conditions eased in the afternoon and evening. With some calmer water we were able to row again and got in a couple of really good sessions, which made us feel much better. The night stayed relatively calm but the moon was late up and then a blanket of cloud rolled in. We couldn't even see the horizon; it just merged with the sea making it disorientating and really hard to navigate.

We'd been having problems with our alarm clocks, which just didn't seem to want to go off at the right time. I overslept a couple of times, something that's unforgivable out at sea where every second of sleep counts. Lin quite rightly wasn't happy and commented on it 'becoming a bit of a habit'. I felt awful about it, but I wasn't doing it on purpose and didn't know how to stop it happening. I also felt it was a bit unfair because I wasn't falling asleep as much as Lin was during the rowing sessions. I thought she could have been a bit more understanding, but decided there was nothing else for it other than to take it on the chin and try a bit harder. The result was that we agreed the rower would shout a 10 minute and 5 minute warning to the person resting so they could get up in time. This seemed to work a treat and immediately put paid to any bad feeling on either side.

Despite the rough and tough conditions, I really was still enjoying the rowing and life onboard our little pink boat. I started to keep my music on all night and it seemed amazing how some songs took on a whole new meaning out there. Even now, hearing them again can move me to tears as I remember listening to them out on the ocean.

> ☒ *John: Just got Cracknells book. Ladies did you not read it?!! Best wishes and I look forward to yours. Keep blogging, John.*

Over the next week we continued our exhausting battle with the elements. We gained great pleasure in clocking up the miles and were heading towards halfway quickly, despite the choppy water. With the cloud cover still persisting most days, naked rowing was on hold and we hadn't been able to run the water maker much. That meant drinking water was the priority so we still couldn't wash our hair or ourselves. We used baby wipes each day to freshen up but that sometimes felt like adding a layer to your skin rather than cleaning it. Our dreadlocks were coming on a treat, but it's not a look that either of us relished. The lack of water for 'luxuries' like washing was quite depressing and meant that Lin actually resorted to plucking her legs in place of shaving!

The skin on our hands and feet started to peel off, and we wondered if it was some kind of extreme exfoliation treatment. Lin suggested that people pay hundreds of pounds for sea salt treatments in spas and here we were getting it for free – until we remembered our £15k entry fee and realised it wasn't so cheap after all! Our bottoms were also extremely sore and covered in painful hard spots (salt sores), dry flaky skin and were bruised from the rowing, although I think the waterproof trousers I'd bought were still proving their worth.

> ☒ *Jen Rudin: Hola Smith & Lin, glad the little row is going well! Just wanted to say a massive well done.*

As the days progressed we were tracked down by support yacht Kilcullen again one morning. Apparently it had taken them all night to find us as we were travelling so fast, and of course our 'stealth boat' status with all our electrics switched off may have contributed to their confusion! It was always great to see the guys, infrequent though their visits were, we treated spotting them like a game, knowing they'd love to creep up and catch us unaware with just our birthday suits on!

Conditions didn't calm any more and we were both running on empty, despite sleeping for as long as we could bear it in our rest periods during the now baking hot days. The moon disappeared again and we were left with some pretty hairy nights in the utter pitch darkness. We'd unconsciously developed a good routine for handovers so we could swap over quickly and efficiently – minimising the time either of us had to be unclipped from the lifelines. We'd decided early on that our rule of always being clipped on outside was a good one. Even so, Lin nearly went over the side during one handover, but just as she reached the point of no return, my arm shot out of its own accord, as fast as a lizards tongue, and hooked onto her harness to steady her at the crucial moment! At times like this we had to trust each other's instincts and reactions implicitly – something we knew was one of our strengths as a team together.

Pete and the crew of Kilcullen

The wind continued to blow from all the wrong places and one night we actually got pushed North 4 miles as well as going West. Several times we wondered whether we should have been out on deck at all but the desire to keep rowing towards our goal was still strong, and we were getting used to Neptune's moods by then.

The dark nights also brought the funniest moment of the trip that far. Just after a handover, I was rowing away when I heard a flapping noise near to where we stored the sea anchor on my left hand side. Thinking that something had come loose in the strong wind, I turned around to see what the problem was, only to find the mother of all flying fish doing its best to commit Hara Kiri on the deck. Lin heard me squeaking, as I tried to pick up the slimy visitor and return it to the sea, so she popped her head out to see what was causing all the noise. To say she found it hysterical was an understatement!

The fish was about 8 inches long and flapping like a good 'un', as I tried to throw it back into the water, especially when I tried to grab its tail to chuck it over the side. Eventually, leaving a trail of slime and dark blue scales, it settled in the foot well of the bow rowing position, stinking to high heaven! Only then was I able to grab the poor, half dead fish and dispatch it back into the sea. Lin was absolutely useless by this point and doubled up laughing at me.

This seemed to herald our arrival well and truly into flying fish country. We never knew that they could get so big or fly so far. Some of them are a beautiful dark blue colour, while others a tad on the grey and ugly side. We used to see them fly over the cockpit of the boat at night, flashing past in the beam of light from our head torches. But we also used to hear other, less lucky flyers have their path interrupted by a little pink rowing boat. Boy those fish must have had big headaches when they smacked into the sides of Barbara Ivy!!

⊠ *Anon: Dear Rachel & Lin, you are two of the bravest people we know! We love your boat! When you win we will be one of the happiest families watching you. Good Luck.*

After 4 weeks at sea we started to suffer physically even more. Lin had some niggly joint pains and I had a headache that wouldn't shift. Even when the water calmed a bit, we worried that it would return to the maelstrom of breaking waves and gale force winds. Nights were harder without the moon light, although sometimes it seemed to be a blessing that we couldn't actually see how big the waves were. We hadn't seen any wildlife for ages and even the Storm Petrels seemed to be keeping a low profile. It seemed eerie with so much cloud around.

⊠ *Mike & Lizzie: Hey girls, great going. We are keeping track of you from Aussie. Sending a helping hand from across the seas and oceans. All the best.*

We saw in the New Year at twelve o'clock UTC (GMT), celebrating with another mini bottle of Champers. But our high spirits were short lived, and we seemed to get it all in one incredibly awful day. Massively huge seas, regular dousings by the waves, and a very strong wind led to very low morale. We both ended up sobbing at different points that day.

Champagne celebration to see the New Year in!

I really missed home right then, and in particular a little ritual that my brother Gordon and I have. Normally we speak to each other just after midnight and he tells me that 'next year you'll be xx years old'. Because my birthday is at the end of the year, this always makes it one higher than the actual next birthday – hence making me seem older than I really am. This time I would have loved to hear him laugh as he mischievously told me I would be 40 next year – but we just couldn't get the phone to connect and I was gutted to miss it.

Lin was in a bad mood from first thing in the morning and inevitably I followed suit eventually. She seemed to be really suffering, both physically and mentally with the constant soakings and her dislike of the splashes and waves were reaching something similar to phobic proportions that day. I asked her what she'd expected it to be like out there, only to find that she had focused so hard on the goal of finishing the race, she'd never actually considered what the 'day to day' might be like.

The day to day was a far cry from my beautiful image of blue sea and sky too and it wasn't really what I'd expected either, but I found I was able to cope by laughing at myself and my preconceived ideas. I just asked myself what on earth had I really expected it to be like? It was the middle of the Atlantic after all! And really, what I'd expected was immaterial; this was what I'd got and there wasn't any alternative. I chose to be there and now it was my choice how I dealt with it. Laughing often seemed as good an option as any!

> ⊠ *Kim: Hi Girls! Think about that more people have been flying in outer space that what you two are doing. You are doing something great. Kim from Denmark.*

On New Years Day I think we probably came the closest to arguing that we did in the entire journey. I was starting to get fed up with Lin's moods and although she'd warned me about them, I had to admit that I never expected them to be so frequent. In the intensity of ocean life, I began to think that it was quite self-indulgent that she allowed herself to be taken over by a mood so regularly, especially as I didn't feel that I was taking the same kind of liberty. But then again, I wasn't suffering in the same way as Lin was and I certainly wasn't in much pain. In fact I was still quite enjoying it out on the water and apart from exhaustion and a few small aches, my body seemed to be bearing up reasonably well.

Lin and her injured foot.

As I went out to row around midday, Lin had clearly been in tears again but she didn't want to talk about it and locked herself in the cabin straight away. I wasn't sure what to do and it seemed that whatever I did or said just added to the problem. Little did I know that things were about to reach crisis point.

121

When Lin reappeared for her next shift she seemed calmer and started to tell me a bit about how she was feeling. As she opened up about how she was struggling so much with the conditions and life onboard, I was shocked and sad to hear that she felt it was crushing her resolve bit by bit and that she might be on the verge of a real breakdown. At that point she hated being out there so much she thought that when it was over, she would never want to speak about it again.

I had no idea that things were quite so bad and it was a terrifying thought. Lin is normally so strong and it made me realise how much I relied on her incredible strength for my own. I still didn't know what to do and everything I tried just seemed to make her more annoyed and resentful. I was also finding it hard to understand because although I was uncomfortable, I simply wasn't hating life out there. In contrast, I felt quite at home.

It was awful to see Lin like that and not be able to do or say anything to help. I wondered what was going to happen next and as I rowed on, I prayed that she would be OK. I had a horrible feeling that we might, ironically, end up in the same position as Debra. But I really didn't want to have to make that decision about continuing alone. We'd gone into it as a team and I didn't want to imagine it finishing in any other way.

Eventually I had to know the answer and when we next swapped over I blurted out a clumsy question, asking probably in a very unsympathetic way whether Lin was thinking about giving up. I was so relieved when the answer was a firm 'no'. Having spent her rest period thinking it through, Lin had decided that she wasn't going to give in that day and told me she was determined to stick it out. But I was still really worried about her deteriorating morale and the disturbing turn of events that day.

Life at sea is an emotional rollercoaster and in a real demonstration of how a day can compact all the extremes of your emotions into just a few hours, we saw our day flip right over a short while later. I was getting ready to go outside and row when Lin called out and asked me to grab a camera. She'd seen a huge, dark shape in the water, first assuming it was some wood or a container lost from a ship, then realising that the 'container' she was trying to avoid, was actually staring right at her, eyeball to eyeball!

The whales had come to visit! Someone has since suggested to us that whales can sense distress, and they may well have a point because it was normally on the days when we were feeling at our lowest ebb when they paid us a visit. On that day, when we were at rock bottom, we saw whales in their natural habitat for the first time in our lives. We were treated to a real show as they checked us out thoroughly, swimming and playing around and right under the boat for over an hour. They'd move away to breathe, and then surf back to us in the big waves. But despite their mammoth proportions we never felt scared or threatened; to us they just seemed very curious and we were enthralled. It was like we were the zoo exhibits and they had come to check out the unusual creatures.

Whale swimming alongside the boat!

At the end of the visit, with what seemed just like a friendly goodbye wave of a side fin – they were gone, leaving us in a much better frame of mind. Amazingly, after they'd left the sea seemed to turn soft and 'marsh-mallowy', and as the boat bobbed along happily the mood on board had changed, becoming distinctly calmer and a lot more positive.

Adding to our strange day, just a bit later on, we saw one of the most bizarre sights of the whole trip – a huge moth! It fluttered in, thought about landing, changed its mind and fluttered off. It was really weird because we were hundreds of miles from land and the moth had nowhere to settle. He must have hitched a lift on a boat or something. He set off towards the west, which meant it was even further to the nearest island and we wondered if he'd make it!

⊠ *Donna Malcolm: Hi girls, fabulous progress. Wipe away the tears in case you miss something amazing. Every inch counts so keep up the excellent work.'*

Chapter 14

The days continued with regular soakings for both of us and some huge, steep waves; steep enough to threaten turning us over if we didn't meet them stern-on. The cloud cover also continued more often than we would have liked, with no sign of a break for several hundred miles. Neither of us was particularly enjoying the experience just then and to add insult to injury, our bottoms were pretty bad from the damp too – a mixture of bruising from sitting on the seat and salt sores in a number of sensitive areas. It felt like sitting on pins and needles sometimes and both our gel seat pads and fluffy covers felt like they had rocks in them. Even our regular application of Sudocrem and baby talc didn't seem to be helping, so we tried various solutions like Aloe Vera gel and Elizabeth Arden 8-hour cream with varying levels of success.

In addition to this our hands and feet were still peeling madly and we felt unbelievably yukky because the lack of sun meant low power and therefore no spare water to wash properly. Our hair was so matted we could hardly haul a brush through the combination of grease and salt water as we tended our new dreadlocks daily! It was amazing how much this affected our morale.

Dreadlocks!

The crazy conditions were exhausting and we were desperate for some sun. The wind was absolutely relentless too – you could hear it whistling constantly, inside and outside the cabin. Even with headphones in and the music up loud, you could still hear it howling and it continued to drive me nuts. It was only then that we found out our tracking beacon had bitten the dust again and was only working when it felt like it. So we had to fiddle around with the fuses for a while, but that did seem to do the trick. While it didn't bother us much whether it was working or not, we knew that everyone at home, religiously checking our position online, would worry like mad again if we didn't seem to be moving.

☒ *Anon 'Hi Girls, been keeping up with your blog &*
just want to wish you Happy New Year. People like
you are giving my Mum hope and strength.'

Lin's low mood continued and she kept talking about just letting the boat drift with both of us in the cabin. My feeling was that the conditions were too extreme. For one I knew our boat would immediately turn broadside to the wind and waves, increasing our risk of capsizing. Even though I also knew the solo boats must have done this all the time, it just didn't sit well with me. I desperately wanted to keep going and get to Antigua as fast as possible. Drifting equated to giving up in my mind and I simply wasn't ready to do that yet.

I guess that it seemed to me like Lin had lost some of her normal fight, or rather, it had been drained out of her. There still didn't seem to be much that I could do to help as I'd tried everything I could think of without success. The constant soakings and battering by the elements were taking their toll.

☒ *Donna Malcolm 'You can't change the weather,*
temperamental thing it is, but you can change how
you feel about it – head up, walking tall. Waves are
your friend.'

But by day 34 (4th January) things did improve slightly. Lin came out from one of her night time breaks with a changed outlook and the bad mood had suddenly lifted. She felt stronger and her fresh resolve carried us both through the night. The waves were still huge and the wind very strong, but we knew we could cope with it and let's face it – what was the option really?!

We also changed the Tesco's bag covering the Nav light for a new advanced prototype light shade - the cut off bottom of a squash bottle! The bag eventually blew away in the wind and Lin had been saving the bottle end for just such a moment. This time we were more prepared for hanging over the forward cabin to reach the light and there were far less bruises involved on Lin's hips! It lifted our spirits as we felt like we'd got one up on Neptune at last!

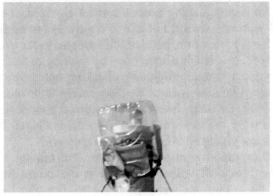

The high-tech light cover!

⊠ *Jo & Lou: Which Baggy Trousered 1980's rapper was half shark? MC Hammerhead. The faster you row, the quicker these awful jokes will cease! You are doing marvellously x.*

The next day the mood lifted again as it was sunny enough to make some drinking water and row naked in an attempt to dry out our now ragged and sore bottoms. We had some music out on deck and I marked up the finish line on the Antigua chart – it was exciting to see even though we were still chasing the halfway point.

As the sun continued we managed to build up our stock of drinking water to 20 litres, the most we'd had since leaving La Gomera. Night times were calmer and full of stars blanketing the sky from horizon to horizon. We were regularly treated to a lightshow of shooting stars across the sky in a range of colours. We made a lot of wishes on those stars!

We had kept our clocks on GMT, which meant that it was staying light until 8.30pm – although that meant dawn happened at around 8.30am, so we weren't getting any additional daylight and often the sun didn't make an appearance until around 10am. We had a few light rainstorms that night and saw lightning from electrical storms in the distance, but the air was distinctly warmer round the ankles and I was thrilled to be able to row in shorts all night for the first time!

⊠ *Hope Afloat: From Hope Afloat, a dragon boat team of breast cancer survivors, Philadelphia USA. You two are awesome. We are watching your progress and send strength to you.*

A friend texted us on Day 36 (6th January) with the sad news that her Mum had breast cancer – she was diagnosed the previous year but was doing well through treatment. We just couldn't believe it, yet it reminded us about why we chose to do the row in the first place and what an impact breast cancer has for the person diagnosed and their friends and family.

We were also getting more texts from Kim who lives on a sailboat in San Francisco Bay. She's the founder and editor of an online boating magazine called YachtPals.com and had questions coming in for us from her readers all over the world!

⊠ *Jo & Lou: Congratulations! You've broken 1,000 miles @ 6pm today! We're having yet another drink in your honour – this rowing malarkey is very tough on our livers! Love J&L.*

At 6pm on the 6th January, we completed 1,000 nautical miles. There were other boats still close by and to the north of our position, but Atlantic Jack had been having more rudder problems. We felt genuinely sorry for the girls and hoped they were safe at least.

⊠ *Pam Newby: 6th Jan 2307h – 1514 left, 1038 done. Nearly halfway. Well done! How are your bums bearing up? Love to you both especially the birthday girl*

January 7th was Lin's birthday, and sunny enough for us to fill up the spare 5 litre ballast bottle that we'd had to drink a few days before when we'd been hand pumping water. We had to carry 150 litres of fresh water as ballast and an emergency supply of drinking water. But if you drank more than 50 litres you incurred penalties, so we were determined to keep our use to a minimum.

It seemed to be an OK day for Lin and she liked her presents but didn't feel up to having any birthday champers. My Mum called on the sat phone to wish her a happy birthday and we also had surprise calls from Sally Kettle and the Jaydubyoo boys. They were also in much better spirits, had been in the water to clean their hull and were rowing hard for Antigua.

Sadly, after a choppy and no doubt painful session, Lin announced that she was in a foul mood. Luckily (for me!) neither the chop nor the mood hung around for long and Lin poured her energy in to working out an estimate for our arrival in Antigua. The best bet was around 30 days, but that was ambitious – as we were to find out.

    ⊠ *Anne & Robert: Hi R&L, I know you are having a rough time out there but believe me we are rooting for you. Our lives revolve around your little green dot.*

With more sun we topped up the water and were even able to fill the pink 'us' bucket and wash some clothes. Our sense of smell seemed to have gone into overdrive in the clean, unpolluted ocean air and the washing detergent smelled lovely. Strangely, we never did notice any horrible body smells like you get on land, even when we were both stuck in the sweatbox of a cabin together. Our clothes developed a slightly musty, salty whiff when they'd been worn for a good few weeks at a time, but there wasn't anything really foul hanging around.

The 9th January (Day 39) was a great day with lots of sun. After our conversation with the Jaydubyoo's on Lin's birthday, we'd checked our hull and sure enough found hundreds of 'critters' growing down the sides, some of which were a couple of centimetres long. It seems that ocean rowing boats provide the perfect home for Goose Neck barnacles to hitch a ride and having so many hangers-on must have been slowing us down a quite a bit as we dragged them through the water.

So, there was only one option – to jump in the water and get rid of the pesky little blighters! After psyching myself up for a couple of hours, I took the plunge and went over the side, armed and dangerous with my pink plastic window scraper, to attack the bottom of the boat. Lin would have done it, but it would have been really unfair to make her jump in as she doesn't like being under the water, and besides, I was actually looking forward to taking a swim in 5,000m of the most intense blue water I've ever seen.

After a slight bikini dilemma where I wondered whether I should put one on (there were fish around!) - the worst bit was slithering over the side and letting go of the gunwales without really knowing how hard it might be to get back in again. It took a while to get my breathing right, but the water was warm and I soon started to enjoy it. The funniest bit was when I got tangled up in my safety rope and wriggled around to shake it away from my legs. All of a sudden, I realised that the rope had come off – I'd obviously tied it on too loosely, probably fine for 'large scale La Gomera Rachel', not realising the mid-Atlantic version was already a bit skinnier!

Barnacle scraping after the bikini dilemma.

Hawkeye Lin stayed on deck to watch out for any stray fins (my early shark warning system), but all she saw was a container ship. There was a huge fish in the water and we thought it might be a tuna, but we didn't really have a clue and couldn't read the label (only joking!). He was blue and yellow and to begin with he was really curious and got a bit too close to my toes for comfort. Until I nearly kicked him on the nose accidentally, when he decided to take a step back.

He was so funny though – every time I scraped some critters loose, he chased off into the blue to catch them and chomp away. Then he'd rush back and sit (or float!) there like a dog begging for food until I scraped off some more! There was barely an inch free of critters and it took about an hour to clear both sides of the hull. I was exhausted afterwards and knew I'd ache the next day. I also bashed my left shin very painfully on the rudder, swallowed a good few mouthfuls of sea water and bumped my head a couple of times. Ah the joys of ocean rowing!

⊠ *Jo Gibson: Hi Rachel & Lin – thinking of you daily and sending treatment vibes to address the aches and pains. You are an awesome pair! Jo (physio).*

But the best bit of the day… I got to have a hair wash and a sponge down to get all the salt off my skin and out of my hair. It was an amazing feeling and made me really appreciate having clean water to wash in every day. Our poor deprived noses went into overdrive when we smelt the shampoo and conditioner too, and we looked like a pair of Bisto kids sniffing the air! But if anyone ever tells you that your hair will self-clean after 6 weeks – please don't believe them. They are lying and it doesn't! There, you now have it on very good, if a little salty, authority!

Swimming in 5,000m of bright blue, crystal clear, Atlantic water.

To finish off a busy day, we had a night time visit from Kilcullen. They'd been hunting us down all day, as it seemed our tracking beacon wasn't working regularly yet again! Lin had just gone inside when I saw bright white, red and green lights in the distance which was really confusing – normally you can only see one or two colours at a time unless something is heading straight for you. Which meant something was heading straight for us! By the time we switched the radio on, they were trying to call us up, so we had to abandon stealth boat and switch everything else on too!

It was really spooky when they came up to us. Kilcullen was creaking and groaning in the dark and sounded like the Black Pearl from Pirates of the Caribbean! Sadly there was no sign of Johnny Depp, just 3 salty old sea dogs trying to make us jealous with tales of the yummy pizza they'd made and eaten earlier! It worked too; our mouths were watering as they sailed away.

☒ *Team Cottle: Two amazing women are rowing like bitches across the Atlantic, hope they don't run out of toilet roll! You are doing brilliantly, excellent progress & we are all very very proud of you both. Syd Squid.*

Chapter 15

Day 40 (10th January) and we'd made it to 37 degrees west after a really fast night – it must have been the barnacle scraping that made all the difference! The boat felt fantastically light and buoyant in the water, which meant much less of a strain on the oars for us. Despite my aches and tiredness from the swim, I felt energised and it was awesome to have clean hair again. Lin even considered going for a dip to try and ease her sore joints, but it was too choppy again and she wasn't really that bothered.

To bring us back to reality, conditions deteriorated over the next couple of days, but even just steering and surfing we made great progress west, covering about 50 miles a day. I had a horrible night around then too when I got up feeling disorientated and unknowingly an hour early for my rowing shift. I was completely dressed and halfway out of the cabin before Lin could point out my mistake and send me back to bed! But then I found I was dozing off while I was outside steering!

We both had some mad dreams when we were sleeping and one night had a very similar hallucination about someone handing something to us, coming to with a start and one arm outstretched while we sat on the rowing seat. It was only the next day we shared the story and realised the spooky similarity. Very strange!

Out at sea, you do tend to spend a lot of time on your own as your rowing partner is generally resting or sleeping when you're rowing. Consequently you're left with plenty of time on your hands to think about life in general and the meaning of the Universe. Or something similar! We both spent some time reflecting on what we'd achieved in our lives so far and thought about what we'd like to do in the future.

Lin seemed to have a much clearer plan than I did, but I certainly saw the row as an opportunity to open new doors. I'd been asked by Audrey, a coaching friend, what I had planned for after the row, but I actually hadn't really thought about it. Instead I wanted to keep all my options open and see what was presented to me in due course. Even then I wasn't sure I'd be able to settle when I'd finished.

I allowed myself one afternoon to think about my Dad. It did cross my mind that if he was alive, then this age of technology and the internet would make tracking people down much easier. I even felt a little shiver as I realised he might even be following our progress right then.

Making our families proud of us had been a key motivator for both of us to do the row – but I will never know whether my Dad is, or was proud of me. On the flip side, whatever the circumstances were, he chose to walk away from a loving family and never came back. In my mind that action had cost him the right to feel proud. I spoke to Lin about it but I wasn't upset. I was just a little sad that wherever he might be he was missing out on his daughters adventure and apart from his disappearance probably triggering my independent streak, he had no part to play in it at all.

⊠ *Janita: Happy New Year from Mousses Bar family in Samos, Greece. Hope this finds you well and that we might see you soon. Will be in UK March. Love Janita*

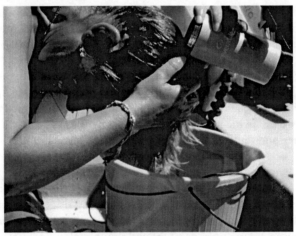

Lin enjoying the luxury of a hair wash!

Lin washed her hair the day after my swim, while I had the horrible job of changing the wheel on my rowing seat. The bearings had rusted which stopped the wheel turning smoothly. It was a really greasy and messy job, but I managed to get all the washers on first time so couldn't complain.

On day 43 (13th January), we were thrilled to pass the halfway mark at last. We had a text from Tony to confirm it and downed our only half bottle of Bolly to celebrate. Halfway was really significant to us as it's something we used in our Dragon Boat racing days. We knew that if we could make it to halfway, we'd already covered the distance, so the second half is only doing the same again. To show how good we both felt that day, we got dumped on by a huge wave and just laughed it off!

The half way bottle of Bolly!

But as in the normal scheme of things, there was some bad news that day too. Lin had been suffering from pain in her left foot since La Gomera when it inexplicably swelled up around her toes while we were working on the boat. At the time we though she'd strained it somehow due to crouching down so much. As it eased, we didn't think she needed medical attention but through the row the pain hadn't disappeared and on reflection it had probably contributed more to the bad moods than I had realised.

Our steering system was simple and therefore easy to fix, with lines leading directly from the rudder, down the outside of the hull before coming inboard and meeting at the left hand side steering shoe. It was very effective and meant that we could react quickly to changing conditions, but it did put a huge burden on your left foot and ankle when it was rough. Which of course was most of the time!

We'd both felt the strain a bit as we had to actively steer and brace the rudder to keep the boat on line but overnight the wind and waves had suddenly whipped the rudder across while Lin was rowing. The result was that the snapping, twisting action did something disastrous to her foot and she was in excruciating pain.

In daylight when we could see properly, it actually looked like she had dislocated her toe. Her whole foot swelled up beyond belief and she was in such a serious amount of pain that it was proving unmanageable.

⊠ Steve Carolan: Hi Rachel, it's Steve Carolan... so proud of you both... past halfway!! GO FOR IT! Xxx

I suggested that Lin spoke to the fleet Doctor to get some advice on what to do and what would be the right kind of drugs to take from the medical kit. Initially not such a good idea, as she snapped back that there wasn't any such thing as a fleet doctor. Even knowing she was in a lot of pain and really worried, I found it hard not to retaliate as I was just trying to help, and I knew there definitely was a doctor. It was only much later on that I found out these comments were prompted by Lin's fear that the doctor would tell her she couldn't continue rowing.

Eventually I dug out the information about the doctor and left it out in the cabin for Lin to find, then suggested she called Tony at HQ for some advice. Then I left it with her and didn't mention it again. She made the call!

⊠ Philippa Campbell: 1/2 way! No turning back now! Stroke by stroke, seat by seat, wave by wave – you'll get there. Aim high!

Advice from the doctor (who was also an ocean rower!) was to start a course of antibiotics in case the swelling was caused by an infection, while trying out different combinations of drugs to manage the pain. So we carried on with Lin using her right foot to steer in the left shoe because her injured foot was so swollen it wouldn't go in the shoe. It wasn't looking good at all.

Meanwhile, I was starting to suffer because the rowing shoes we used were two sizes too big for me. We had to order them to fit Lin who is two sizes bigger, and thought I'd get away with it although my feet are so much smaller. But I developed large, deep and nasty pressure sores on my heels and the side of my toes. They were incredibly painful and it got far worse when Lin swapped her foot over to steer as it stretched the left shoe even more. By day 44 (14th January), for the first time since we set off, I just wanted to get to Antigua as fast as possible.

We started to get a lot more rain, particularly at night and neither of us had any dry clothes again. After Lin had spoken to the doctor she seemed very down, which was only to be expected as she was in so much pain, her foot was very swollen and she couldn't bear any weight on it. The antibiotics continued and any small improvement would have indicated an infection and therefore a cure. But there was no improvement, which suggested the cause was an injury requiring rest to heal and of course rest was the one luxury we couldn't have on the ocean.

    ☒ *James Crawford: Hey how's it going? Tired? Bored? Have you played I-spy yet? Keep it up, you two are mental.*

We did try I-spy for a while, but quickly came to the conclusion that far too many things at sea begin with 's'. Sea, sky, seat, sheepskin, sleeping bag, stars, salt… you get the picture!

By the time we made it to 040 degrees west - with 20 degrees (1,200 nautical miles) left to go, I started worrying about making the finish line. It was a silly niggling worry, but the finish line was only one nautical mile long and with the Northern end touching Antigua, there was very little room for manoeuvre as we got closer. I was concerned that we seemed to be travelling too far south too soon. The weather typically wasn't due to change, so we decided to do what we could to try and reduce our southern progress a bit.

But it wasn't to be and on a particularly rough night it was clear we couldn't carry on in this relentless way. Lin was in agony and it wasn't fair to push either of us so hard. We tied everything down, climbed into the cabin together and drifted along for the rest of the night. Lin was in so much pain, she couldn't really row at all, and I'd reached a point where I was too tired to put up a fight with the ocean. I really didn't want to drift, but right then it felt like there really wasn't any other option. In my mind it seemed like I'd given up and I didn't want to feel like that. But I did know deep down that it was the right decision. I also knew that while I could have continued on the 2-hour shifts, I couldn't do it alone – this challenge still needed both of us.

Lin reminded me that before we set off we'd promised ourselves that if it got too much we would rest and look after ourselves. We'd talked about how decisions made on any particular day could affect our ability to continue tomorrow, in a week or even a month's time. I had a responsibility as half of the team to make sure we continued to work together towards our mutual goal. In this case it meant a sacrifice on my part, or at least a perceived sacrifice, but also meant that Lin had to help me cope with the disappointment that I was feeling in addition to the pain that she was in.

135

It was very uncomfortable cooped up in the cabin together, but in all honesty it wasn't quite as bad as we'd expected. It was no worse than being on sea anchor anyway, and the rest did do us both good! We left the Sea-me, GPS and AIS on all night, together with the automatic bilge as we weren't able to bail the foot well quite so regularly. Luckily the batteries lasted the night and I woke myself up regularly to scan the horizon for any stray ships heading in our direction. Bizarrely we made brilliant progress and actually drifted 18 miles West and 4 miles North. We laughed as we wondered why we were even bothering going out on deck to row or steer when sitting in the cabin getting some extra sleep could produce such great mileage!

After our enforced rest overnight we carried on steering and surfing through the next day. Lin was really struggling to row with the bad foot, so it was probably for the best that we weren't rowing. Eventually the conditions calmed right down and we actually had a wonderful night that we could both enjoy.

☒ *Jason Hart (our boat's former owner): How's that emotional rollercoaster going? Doing fantastic. Look forward to getting under 1,000 mls. Enjoy enjoy, nothing compares. Jas Hart.*

There was a half moon up, lighting our way until 4am and the stars were out all night. There were just a very few tiddly little clouds around. It was just an amazing night to be out on the ocean and we were able to start rowing again by morning, hitting 042 degrees West just before daylight. The upbeat mood continued and we had music on deck and enough water for a hair and body wash each, which was sheer bliss. Even Lin was able to row as the conditions were good enough for her to manage the steering. Meanwhile I was taking advantage of the calmer water to administer some self-physio. My ribs, which I've had long term problems with, had been stiffening up, but I found a way to manipulate them and fix them myself, by lying back on my knuckles made into a fist!

As it was such a great day for jobs requiring no waves, I stuck my head out of the stern inspection hatch and lengthened the spare steering line. The main line was fraying where it caught on a scupper cover and we'd need to change over to our spare line if it snapped. Then I changed the Spanish courtesy flag for the Antiguan one – possibly a bit early, but worth doing while we had the chance without getting any water in our sacred dry haven - the cabin!

Heading into the last 1,000 miles.

The rainstorms started to get worse as we headed into the tropics and on 18th January (Day 48) I got drenched during the night, decided enough was enough and headed inside. Again it felt strange to 'give up' again and I still didn't like the feeling, but it was pointless to stay sitting outside just getting wet and miserable. So we sat it out inside and waited for the rain to pass while we grabbed a couple of extra hours sleep and drifted in the right direction.

By morning the water looked really strange after the storm in the night – very slick and shiny, like mercury, but it was also very sluggish and hard to row in. A shoal of fish followed us for a while and we could see them clearly in the water. We were down to 30-35 miles per day, which was really disappointing, but we couldn't do anything other than keep on rowing. Lin was still using her right foot in the left shoe and doing a great job, although a side effect was that she was starting to feel pain in her right Achilles due to the strain of steering with the opposite foot.

But despite all the challenges, our sense of humour was still there and we found we could laugh at most things – like the night I was late waking Lin up to take over the rowing shift, but only because I was too busy trying to work out whether the big cloud I could see looked more like a monkey face or Bart Simpson!

    ☒ *Navigation News: Hi, just wanted to say you two are awesome, doing this for Breast Cancer Care. It's not much I know, but I'm putting you in my magazine 'Navigation News.*

Day 49 pushed us further south than we really wanted, but we were thrilled to hear that Pura Vida was the first boat to finish this year's race. We were so pleased to hear about it, but thought it ironic we were so far behind them and getting excited about being within 24 hours of reaching the magical 1,000 miles to go mark. We took the symbolic step of folding out our last section on the chart. We only ever had a small section visible because it made our daily progress seem so much greater and unfolding the whole of the Atlantic was simply too overwhelming. Later on Hilary texted to tell us that when she did two zooms in on the web site map she could see land now! Antigua was in sight.

Antigua this way!

⊠ *Rupert Saunders: Fantastic that you are still there and shite that the weather has turned nasty again. Just think of the beaches, the rum punch and a bed!*

The southerly progress continued – far too fast, and the rain kept coming down. Both of us were getting regularly soaked, but then the hot sun would come out again, so we resorted to sitting out there in just our jackets with nothing underneath!

Spirits rose again as we passed the 1,000 miles to go mark and we celebrated in a highly decadent fashion with champers in the morning! We figured it must be champagne o'clock somewhere on the planet! Overnight we'd only dropped south by one mile, but gained a massive 20 miles west. So we took the decision to sit it out entirely that day, as we actually couldn't row much faster than 20 miles in 12 hours anyway. This would give Lin a great opportunity to rest her legs and we could catch up on some much needed maintenance.

⊠ *Gordon: By the time you get this you will be under the 1,000nm to go stage. Congratu-flippin-lations! Hope the bubbly tastes even better now! Luv G&D.*

Our entertainment for the lazy day consisted of GPS watching, fun with our sticker and puzzle books, jokes from our joke books, Radio 1 podcasts, sleep, GPS watching, commenting on the weather, chatting, listening to music and GPS watching! We both really wished we were in Antigua by then, but at least we'd made the magical move into 3-digit miles to go! It felt really strange to be sitting around; I felt kind of guilty; but the wind was really strong and we were going in the right direction for once.

We spoke to Elin and Herdip on Dream Maker, who were about 32 miles ahead of us. They told us that they spent 30 hours battling to row South over the last few days, only to get blown North again as soon as they rested. It sounded like the trip wasn't quite what they expected and we felt strangely comforted by that. The girls had been advised to stay further north, but then Jon and Nick who were way ahead of us on No Fear told them not to worry too much about going south. It was all very confusing and we weren't sure we agreed!

During our lazy day drifting we covered over 36 miles and our southerly progress seemed to slow down at last. We spoke to Elin & Herdip again and they were doing OK. They drifted overnight too, but made a few miles on us. It was so good to talk to them and we agreed to keep in touch every couple of days because it boosted morale for all of us while it was so tough out there.

We heard that Bill & Pete our South Africans buddies and No Fear (Jon and Nick) had finished and there were other teams very close to Antigua. Jon and Nick did end up going really far south and still said not to worry, but then Sally texted us to say we should row northwest as soon as possible. We wondered what on earth was going on?!!

⊠ *Philippa Campbell: Following your every stroke. Focus on 1 task at a time during the bad weather. I know your determination will get you to the finish line! Aim for the sun!*

By day 52 (22ⁿᵈ January) we were still being pushed South by the current, had North-Easterly winds and a swell from the North, all of which resulted in a criss-cross of yukkiness for us.

But we were bored of drifting and steering, so we conducted a highly technical experiment of 'drifting versus rowing', with the steering locked on. The conclusion was that we should row, but we switched to rowing in 1-hour shifts. It was all we could manage against the wind and waves and was unbelievably horrible. Every single stroke was a strain and we felt our joints stretching and popping as we forced our oars through the water. It was really hard, unrelenting work and reminded us of paddling the dragon boats at Peterborough, a very shallow regatta course where it feels like you're hauling the boat through treacle. We found it was too exhausting and painful to do more than one hour at a time and literally collapsed in a heap in the cabin after every shift.

Although Lin's foot was a bit better after the rest, the conditions weren't doing her any favours and we now had waves breaking over the front of the boat, soaking us from behind too. So we battened down again for the night and wondered if we'd end up in Barbados instead of Antigua. We'd heard it was quite nice that time of year, but our finish line was Antigua and that's where we wanted to go. As we settled down, all I could hear was Lin laughing at my comedy wails of "but I don't want to go South" as I gazed at the GPS ticking off our southerly progress.

The laughter didn't last long because we drifted 7 miles South in the night and when we realised, we were devastated. But what were the options? All we could do was take a deep breath, grab the oars and set about clawing it back again. To add injury to insult, I'd slept badly on my neck and was in some pain, but managed to manipulate it back into place myself. It was extremely tricky as the boat bounced around, but I thought my physio, Jo, would have been proud of me!

> ⊠ *Becky Jesse: Have been reading about your journey! Well done both! I know you've got what it takes! Love Becky.*

It took 11 hours of solid rowing to go just 1 mile north the next day. It was so hard pulling against the wind and waves, knowing all the time that the minute we stopped rowing we would immediately lose the hard earned distance. But we had to believe that a mile gained today was one less that we'd have to claw back the next. Everything ached – our hands, elbows, shoulders, backs, hips, knees and feet. On every stroke we could literally feel our joints separating and pulling apart under the pressure.

Our mood was low again. Lin's foot was holding up, but still very painful and we both got soaked a couple of times an hour, which was no fun. The only relief was a phone call from the Jaydubyoo boys who told us they really were too far south now and were desperately trying to get further north. We felt sorry to hear they were having a rough time too, but it did give us some confidence that our ongoing battle really was necessary and would eventually pay off for us.

   ☒ *Suzy Wadsworth: Hey girls, just checked your position and I can see Antigua on the same bit of map now!! You are so close. Good luck for the home straight.*

24th January (Day 54) started really well as we found we'd only drifted just over 1 mile South during the night and we made that back in around 2 hours of slog. We finally arrived back up at 59 degrees north again by 7pm but just before we handed over, Lin popped her head out of the cabin to let me know that despite rowing virtually due north, we were actually still travelling south. It was devastating news after all the hard work and I sat there feeling empty and tearful. I hated the thought that I was letting everyone down – Lin, all our supporters and myself. It brought all the self-doubts I had about being the weaker rower flooding back.

But when Lin took over she also struggled to make progress North, which did actually make me feel a bit better about my own ability! After battling it for a while she suggested that we stop early and get a good nights sleep ready to launch an attack again early in the morning when we were well rested. While the one-hour shifts did seem to work better for us physically in these heavy conditions, we both found that we preferred the 2-hour routine and hoped that we could get back into it soon. We shared our frustrations with those at home via the blog and appealed for everyone to do a kind of 'Uri Geller' thing at a set time to send us 'go West' vibes. We were prepared to try anything!

   ☒ *Gordon: Hi both. We did our thing for you at 12pm. In fact all of my office and friends did! Hope it helped. Not long to the 850nm now! Keep going. G&D*

By now we had just 900 miles to go and we desperately wanted to finish. Our 30-day estimate from two weeks before now seemed miles out, unless of course we were on the receiving end of a miracle and the conditions changed to help us a bit more! So when we spotted a sail in the distance there was great excitement onboard and we thought it might be Kilcullen. Lin called out on the radio and ended up in contact with a US sail boat, sailing from La Gomera to Antigua! We had a nice chat with a very friendly fellow who offered to buy us a beer in Antigua when we arrived, if he was still there then!

After the tears of the previous day, my frustration deepened further when we drifted 4 miles south again in the night. Every time I woke up I'd obsessively check the GPS, which was on my side of the cabin, only to see the numbers ticking down depressingly as we headed in the wrong direction. We spoke to Tony at HQ again and he thought we might be caught up in an eddy – a huge swirl of water hundreds of miles across that behaves much like an eddy in a fast moving river. What we'd been experiencing over the last few days didn't match the weather reports, although other boats reported similar bizarre conditions at the same time as us, even though they were over 100 miles away.

Tony's advice was to stay above 16 degrees 30 minutes North; otherwise he thought we might struggle to get back to the right latitude later on. We weren't quite sure how we were going to do it, and we were getting too exhausted to fight so relentlessly, so I agreed with Lin's suggestion that we just row West for a day and see what happened. As we rowed on the positive note was that it was sunny and the batteries reached an all time high of 13.6v of charge – so we made extra water and washed our hair as a treat! Happy days!

Back in La Gomera before the start, another rower had told us that eddy's normally last for 7 days, and when we remembered this we hoped it would mean we were near the end of this one. We crossed our fingers, (as well as you can when rowing!) and changed back to 2-hour sessions. Amazingly, towards the end of my first 2-hour session, Lin spotted that we were slowly travelling North again. At first I didn't believe her, but progress continued right through the night and we kept on rowing to take advantage of the helpful current.

Around that time we saw a really odd ship a couple of miles away from us. It was odd because it took a while to respond on the VHF and it appeared to have its AIS switched off which meant that we couldn't identify it. When we eventually made radio contact and had a short, rather abrupt conversation, the AIS ID suddenly appeared for a few minutes, then disappeared again completely. It was really strange. The ship did change course slightly to avoid us, but they didn't bother calling back to confirm. We wondered why they were trying to be a 'stealth boat' when they were so big and speculated about what they might have had on board!

By noon the next day, we'd made it to 17 degrees north and 047 degrees west. Conditions remained tough, but we found that if I locked off the steering, Lin could still row across the waves without any pressure on her injured foot. This worked really well until we needed to bear towards the West and therefore steer the boat stern on to the waves. The locked steering only worked when the boat was broadside and I needed to be more reactive when we were stern on to stop her swinging from one extreme to the other.

Lin rowing with her right foot in the left shoe.

I untied the ropes and found it was much better for me, but then Lin was finding it impossible to steer with her foot due to the pain. I struggled to find a solution that was good for both of us and know Lin felt just as frustrated because all my suggestions were batted aside. Eventually I tied up a broken bungee into knots and clipped it round the footplate to absorb any sharp movements from the rudder while still allowing some controlled movement of the shoe when it was needed. This seemed to work and thankfully, our little friend eddy seemed to have buggered off and left us alone at last! Things were looking up.

 ⊠ *Philippa Campbell: Spirits sound high on BI – well done both of you! Great news about the wind direction – positive thoughts do work! Heads down and listen for the Cavalry. Love P.*

Day 57 (27th January) was a brilliant day. There was literally not a single cloud in the fabulous blue sky and both the wind and waves, and therefore us, were Antigua bound. It felt like we were the Antigua Express and really motoring along! We also had visitors of the human kind. Having spotted another sail early in the morning, we got on the radio as normal and made contact with a catamaran (we think it was called Astaria), with two German and two French blokes onboard, heading to Martinique. After a chat, they went on their way, only to radio back 5 minutes later to ask permission to come over and take some pictures as they'd never seen an ocean rowing boat before.

The funny thing was that I'd just finished on the bucket and Lin was about to commence her morning ablutions. We both panicked as we didn't have many clothes on and got in a bit of a tizz with all the excitement of visitors dropping by. I rushed to take over the oars and get dressed all at the same time – and believe me, it's impossible to put shorts on while sitting on a rowing seat. So while I was falling all over the deck, Lin got tangled up in her harness and safety line – spinning round and round to untangle herself, as the catamaran got ever closer.

Without going into too much detail, it was not the most relaxing time Lin ever spent on the bucket! But we were both present and correct as our visitors arrived a safe distance away and did a loop round us, clicking away on their cameras. Freddie the skipper was on his 5th Atlantic crossing and was amazed – he'd never seen two blondes in a pink boat before!

We started to get some pressure from home to give an ETA for Antigua as bookings for flights and accommodation were going up in price daily. Normally teams wait until they have around 500 miles to go, but things were looking complicated and expensive for our supporters. Tony's calculations were similar to ours, so we took a chance and decided we could realistically expect to arrive in Antigua any time from 16-20 February. We gave them the go ahead and the bookings machine swung into action. It was all really exciting.

> ⊠ *Gordon: Sitting here scoffing my first cream egg*
> *of 2008. Will have one waiting for you when you get*
> *back. If yer good, maybe even mini-eggs! Luv G&D.*

We'd settled back into the 2-hour sessions really well and were finding it warm enough to just sleep in our clothes, without any sleeping bags at last. We just added a jacket when we went outside at night and rowed in as little clothing as possible in the day. The miles were ticking away, daytime temperatures were increasing, and all thoughts were on getting to Antigua and relieving our multiple aches and pains.

Chapter 16

The rain kept coming back in short sharp showers that sent us bolting for shelter at various times of the day. But we were getting really good at timing it to perfection. Often the wall of water would be just about hitting the stern of the boat as whoever was rowing would yell 'incoming' and dive inside for cover. We also both caught each other staring at the sky in utter confusion as frequently we'd see and feel rain falling, only to look up and find a cloudless blue sky directly above. We really couldn't work that one out but at least it made us both laugh at our bemused faces looking skyward!

We noticed that our daily texts were reducing in number and wondered if everyone was starting to forget about us because we'd been out there so long – only to get one from Debra to say she wanted to try and get to the finish to see us in. Sadly work commitments prevented her from making the trip, but just knowing that she'd wanted to be there meant the world to us.

We also got a very exciting message from Caroline at Antigua & Barbuda Search and Rescue, the team who escorts the race boats across the finish line.

> ⊠ *Caroline: You are doing amazingly well ladies, keep rowing, positive, strong. We await your arrival here in Antigua – great respect and admiration for you. Caroline (rescue boat).*

We were beside ourselves with excitement now, but there was more to come and we nearly burst when we heard from home that flights were booked and our accommodation in Antigua was to be a self-catering villa with a pool no less! We couldn't wait to hear all the details about the luxury pad – and kept popping our heads out of the cabin to yell 'villa with a pool' at each other. We had definitely been out at sea for far too long! But we were sad to hear that Jo and Lou couldn't make it to Antigua in the end; it was a huge shame after all they'd done to support us.

Day 60 (30th January) brought a little light relief in the form of 'Twickers', a massive turtle with a head the size of a rugby ball. It was another hot, sunny day and the happy mood onboard continued when we passed the 50 degrees West mark at last. In the afternoon we took a break from rowing so Lin could paddle her sore feet in the cool water and try to reduce the swelling – until a small shoal of little fish came along to take a look and her dangling toes were swiftly retracted! As it was such a beautiful day and relatively calm for once, I took the opportunity to jump in for a swim and cleaned the bottom of the boat again.

This time I was accompanied by four little yellow and blue fish friends. They turned out to be quite pushy chaps and kept swimming right in my face to grab at the pickings. I tried to grab them too, but they were far too quick for me. I loved being back in the water again and afterwards we both had a good scrub down and hair wash. It felt fantastic to be so clean. The water stayed calm enough for Lin to row and despite our time off the oars, we made great mileage.

Freshly washed hair!

A text from Jen, the land support for our buddies onboard 'The Reason Why' made us laugh.

☒ *Jen: It's good to be a woman rower! Seen photos of Steve/Paul @ finish with their beards – not a pretty sight!! Least you won't have that problem – I hope!*
Ha ha, Jen x.

We heard that we were last in the pairs class now, but only just behind Dream Maker and it looked like being a fast race overall. But knowing that we were only 24 miles from being three quarters of the way to Antigua and our next little bottle of champers kept us happy enough.

After all our efforts to keep North in the previous days and weeks, we actually drifted 15 miles above our ideal latitude a couple of nights later. We hoped it wasn't going to be another out and out battle. But we managed to row 7 miles South during the day and hoped that nature would co-operate with the rest over night. We continued rowing for most of the night, but stopped part way through as Lin was in a lot of pain again and the conditions were making it too dangerous to be out on deck. So we settled back down for an extended rest until daylight.

Apparently, while we were tucked up and fast asleep we overtook Dream Maker – and the girls got in touch in the morning to find out why we didn't stop for a cup of tea as we floated on by. It was really funny because we had no idea we were travelling so well. I'd been setting the rudder as best I could if we did go inside at night, trying to use the angle of the wind catching the cabin to our advantage and imagining how the boat would behave if she had a sail. But I think it was really our superior boat design that meant we could just slip through the water!

We also found out that there were a few boats further West and South stuck on sea anchor in stormy weather. Niall and James in Komale had only managed 9 miles in 3 days, which must have been awful for them - to be so close to Antigua, yet so far away.

⊠ *Orlando Rogers (Go Commando): To my two favourite rowing chicks, loving the photos and blogs, the pair of you seem in excellent spirits. Antigua is a paradise (nearly) and worth it. Love Orlando.*

Kilcullen paid us a final visit, but couldn't get too close due to the huge swell as they told us they were heading in to Antigua very soon. Meanwhile our plans for Antigua were progressing well and we just had to make sure we arrived in there after the 16th February to meet everyone. But we were starting to realise that if we kept going at the same rate every day, we were going to have to think about slowing ourselves down with the sea anchor, unless of course our buddy Neptune had more up his sleeve to throw at us!

⊠ *Ned Skelton: Well done both in managing your great relationship – exactly as you had planned on 22nd April 2006. What a team!*

Day 63 (2nd February) was really rough all day so we mostly just steered. The wind was very strong again and we got wet all the time, from both waves and rain squalls. We soon learnt that there really isn't a pot of gold at the end of a rainbow… just more rain! The rainbows were amazing though, massive arcs of vivid colour stretching right over us.

⊠ *Amanda Huttley: We're watching you from NZ.*

*Think you're amazing – true British Babes! Telling
all our Kiwi friends.*

We did our best to keep spirits up though – by shouting our new
catchphrase 'villa with a pool!' on a regular basis. And swearing
at the Ocean! With great respect for genuine sufferers, we seemed
to have developed a previously undiscovered form of Tourettes
syndrome, which we named 'Ocean rowing tourettes'. We just
couldn't stop swearing. We regularly found ourselves using words
we would never normally dream of saying. Then when we got
bored of those, we listened to a rap song and found some new ones
to use! We did hope things would switch back to normal without
too much effort once we reached land!

In the morning I was lucky enough to receive a special delivery
from Neptune - a huge wave right over my head. It drenched me
from top to toe and as I sat there gasping, with water dripping off
my face and chin, Lin could only laugh helplessly at the soggy
mess in front of her and throw a towel over. Later on though it
was her turn. I'd just got the video out to do some filming and as I
opened the hatch, heard the warning shout of 'Wave!'

She got soaked! But the video caught the before and after
images, with the camera getting thrown around violently in
between, when the wave hit! All you can hear on the film is the
sound of gallons of water draining off the deck and Lin screaming
with laughter.

Despite our best efforts, we still went two miles south that
night. We spoke to the Jaydubyoo boys again and found they'd
been stuck in the storm for four days and were still 250 miles out
– they were so disappointed as they'd expected to be in Antigua
with their family by this time. They were struggling to steer in
the horrible conditions, so we suggested that they tried our trick
of locking off their steering and rowing with it fixed in position.
They hadn't tried it before and phoned back later on to say that it
had worked really well for them. It was a great feeling to know
we'd been able to help.

   ☒ *Paul and Steve, The Reason Why: Hi Girls, keep
   rowing hard. It will all be worth it when you get here
   to Antigua. The welcome was great and yours will be
   the same.*

The next morning we were woken up early by the VHF radio –
and heard half of a very funny conversation between Dream Maker
and a French solo yacht. It was only the Frenchman's half of the

conversation because he was in range but the girls weren't. From what we could work out it seemed that he'd almost run them over, narrowly avoided hitting them and then got completely confused by the concept of an ocean rowing boat. The girls phoned us later on and told us what a fright they'd had – they woke up to find his boat sitting closer to theirs than the support yachts get!

As he wasn't on deck, they tried to radio him and thought about setting off flares, but he wouldn't have seen them as he was inside. In the end he was so close they resorted to yelling and shouting to wake him up and get him to change course. He literally missed them by just a few feet. The funniest thing was that he couldn't work out what kind of boat they were in and we heard him ask 'are you some sort of dinghy?!' in a bemused French accent!

⊠ Caroline (ABSAR): 550 miles left, you're AMAZING – Pink Power! Might have to breathalize your entrance of E Harbour. Perfect position, hope foot OK. Keep SAFE, very strong. Caroline x.

We were gutted to find that we'd drifted to 16 degrees, 54 minutes North over night, which was the furthest South that we'd been. So, in horrible conditions we had to try to go North yet again, across the wind and waves. We made good progress West, but it was just so slow, painful and demoralising. Added to the foot problems, Lin was really suffering from her salt sores again, which made it doubly difficult for her when she was rowing. The only positive point was that in our exhausted state we slept quite well for a change and even the messages beeping as they came in on the phone didn't wake us up!

⊠ Jan - Lin's Mum: 527 @ 2305. You really must have some champagne when you reach 500. No! No! I insist. Save some for when you first spy land soon.

We battled all day and the conditions were a bit easier in the afternoon, but we finally had to give up as it was too dark (no moon), and we were regularly taking a hit, sideways on, by some massive waves. We had only made back half a nautical mile North all day, which was unbearably depressing. But we just kept on telling ourselves that it was half a mile in hand for the next day, all the time knowing that we were still drifting further South. The only highlight was reaching the 500 miles to go point and consoling ourselves with a glass of champagne.

Our grapevine told us that Atlantic Jack had to take on a resupply, which meant they were disqualified from the race. It was a real shame; we would have hated to be in that position ourselves and felt really sorry for the two girls onboard. They'd overcome some huge problems to get that far.

⊠ *Emma and Steve: Following progress with sons Josh 5 & Jake 3. Re-enacting hull cleaning & radio messages. Keep going girls. Best wishes.*

That night we slept better again, even missing the text messages for a second night in a row! But we were confused to find that we'd changed direction in the night and travelled North instead of South. When we plotted our morning position we found it was actually further north than we'd been for the whole of the previous day's rowing! With this discovery and overtaking Dream Maker, we were starting to wonder whether we should just stay inside and sleep, as we seem to travel faster in the right direction when we did!!

As we got going again, Elin and Herdip called and this time they sounded really desperate. They seemed to be stuck in some sort of horrible squally storm but we were only about 5 or 6 miles away in front of them and couldn't see anything unusual on the horizon behind us. Despite having stayed North of our position for so long, something had pushed them much too far South, and they were starting to worry that they wouldn't be able to get back again.

Lin had a really bad day too. By now, every time she got splashed it triggered off her salt sores again and was excruciating, like sitting on spikes and chunks of rock salt. So all I could hear in my rest periods was lots of noise as she screamed at the sea in her sheer pain and frustration. This time though, I got mad too. The screaming and shouting meant that I couldn't sleep and get a decent rest, but I appreciated how Lin was feeling too. So when I got on the oars, I put my own frustration into rowing as hard as I could and getting us North once more.

After about half an hour, Lin popped her head out to say she knew I was mad at her because we were tanking along and actually travelling North for a change! But as I explained, I hadn't been mad at her – because I could only imagine how much pain she was in from all her sores and injuries. I was just mad because I missed my rest, which wasn't really fair on me. Either way, it worked out really well because we finished the day's rowing at 16 degrees 57 minutes north – spot on target for Antigua. It was good job too because Mum confirmed she'd booked our flights home for 28th February!

⊠ *Emma Finn: Never mind the water ballast, what about the 'Champagne Ballast?! Your boat must be loads lighter now! Drive for the line. Love Emma xxx*

We were also treated to another fabulous visit from some whales. We had seen whales plenty of times in the distance since their first appearance on New Years Day, but this time they stayed and entertained us for about half an hour. They were massive; about 30 feet long and way bigger than the boat. We could see them surfing towards us, a huge dark mass in the clear water, before they'd break out fast and circle round and under the boat. It was amazing to see them play and as they kept on coming back to check us out we got some great pictures. Again we never felt threatened by the whales, big as they were. They always seemed genuinely interested in our little boat and just curious about the strange visitors to their home environment.

Tuesday 5th February meant we'd been at sea for 66 days. We'd made 26 miles on Dream Maker the previous day and could only guess they'd either been on anchor or concentrating on making northerly progress. We hoped they were bearing up OK but it had been an uncomfortable night and we were quite worried about Elin and Herdip. We wanted to call and check on them, but didn't want to sound like we were boasting about getting so far ahead. In the end I just had to man it up and made the call so that we could find out and put our worries to rest. Happily they were fine and told us they'd spent all the previous day working out the right heading and then battling their way North which explained the lack of speed West.

⊠ *Philippa Campbell: Great news that you go faster sleeping than rowing – can you just sleep until 16th? Just kidding! Hope weather holds. Keep focused on that finish line!*

The day progressed into a bad afternoon. Lin was in a lot of pain again and I got upset when we were pushed from N16.58 to N16.54 (4 miles South) in just a couple of hours, despite a huge effort to row North. Eventually, after a handover when Lin made some headway after my pathetic efforts, I just sat and cried at the frustration of it all. I felt like I was letting Lin down because I just couldn't pull the boat North and the fears about being the weaker rower flooded back yet again. It got worse overnight too when we drifted a long way South again to N16.45 degrees – fifteen miles off our ideal latitude. We wondered what on earth we were going to have to do to make it to Antigua, and how much more we could take from Neptune.

> ⊠ *Gordon: Mmmm pancakes! Are we having another pancake day when you get back? Banana and Palm Honey from La Gomera is amazing. Cream Egg later! Luv G&D.*

Day 67 (6th February) and despite starting off so far South, we'd pulled ourselves back together and spirits were better onboard, even if the conditions were still truly awful. We spoke to Dream Maker and they had made it back to N17 degrees but were now 34 miles behind us and had decided to concentrate on staying at that latitude.

The chat with the girls boosted us and proved that as they were finding, persistence would pay off. We know we can both be pretty persistent, now we just had to show it. As our great sailing friend Stu White often tells us, it was time to pull our fingers out! We got back on the oars and planned to go right through the night again, focusing on completing the 40 miles West each day that we needed in order to arrive in Antigua on 16th February.

After my success with other 'fix-it' jobs onboard, I decided to be a little creative and made Lin a sort of 'spray deck skirt' out of carrier bags and duct tape. The idea being that it would deflect the saltwater away from her sore butt and give her a break from some of the discomfort. We'd laughed about it earlier, but it did seem like a good idea as our jackets ended at just the wrong height and were directing salt water into the seats rather than away from them. So, I got a length of cord, duct-taped some of our branded Atlantic Rowing Challenge bags together and handed the stylish garment to Lin for product testing. Although the bags sometimes got trapped in the wheels and runners, it really seemed to work and actually did make a big difference! It became an essential part of her kit for going out on deck, even to sit and cook, and worked so well that I made one to a slightly different design for myself – with a slightly more ruffled finish!! That's high fashion on the high seas for you!

I wasn't finding it such a breeze by now and was suffering with painful ankles, hobbling out of the cabin for my rowing sessions doing a fair impression of Lin. My left ankle, which was the one used for steering, was far worse than the right and I found it painful to stand up, especially if I'd been sitting or lying in the cabin for any length of time. My salt sores were getting out of control again and spreading over a bigger area. Antigua was calling louder.

⊠ *Sam Jones: Hi Rachel, nearly there now!! Keep rowing! I bet you can almost taste that large rum waiting for you at the finish line too.*

The night time rainstorms continued to soak us and the wind remained at over 25 knots with the waves drenching any parts that the rain had missed. It was horrible and we were miserable, but determined to keep battling on. We made back the 15 miles that we needed to go North and had less than 400 miles to go west, but we were fed up, exhausted and emotional. Even I was close to tears several times and that was pretty unusual.

⊠ *Debra Searle: The last few hundred miles will go so quickly. Try not to wish them away as you will ironically miss it when you are home! Savour every moment, even the bad bits. DS.*

My aunt and uncle flew out to Antigua that day and it was exciting to think that John (Lin's dad), Liam and my Mum would be soon too. We couldn't see planes from the sea as they were too high up, but we were excited to imagine what they were all up to as they packed and prepared.

As we got closer to the Caribbean we saw a few more ships. Most had been friendly enough, but we particularly fell in love with a Russian (we think!) Captain on a ship called Ice Fern. He kindly sent a look out to spot us as we weren't showing up on his radar and then changed course to avoid coming too close. That was definitely the kind of treatment we liked!

⊠ *Roger & Amanda: Incredible grunt work Girls, not sure I should be saying this but I've been thinking a lot about your bottoms. Wishing them well too. Luv Rog xx*

By 8th February (Day 69) we were on our knees with exhaustion. Conditions weren't changing and it was clear that we were going to be pushed to the limit in these last few days on the ocean.

As we got closer to land the wildlife increased and we made some new friends. We'd been followed from about 700nm out by a beautiful bird, who we called 'Big White Bird' – mainly because he was big… and white! He used to visit us around the same time every evening and would circle around the boat before coming in to hover just above the rowers' head. Then he'd look down, almost as if he was checking up on us, before he flew off. It really felt like he was coming over to make sure that we were OK and we looked forward to his daily visit. As we ticked off the miles we saw big black and brown birds which all seemed very curious about our little pink boat. While in the water we spotted some huge and very colourful fish who followed the boat along for hours at a time.

The waves were as big as ever and very steep which brought with it a certain nervousness about pitch poling – flipping the boat head over heels. We'd made a conscious decision to wear our harnesses all the time while on deck and our research had shown that most boats that capsize do so once they're within the final third of their crossing. So we reminded ourselves to stay alert and not become overly complacent at this late stage.

The threat of turning head over heels became very real on one day when I was rowing and Lin was inside the cabin. A massive wave rose up behind us, and as it broke around us, we found ourselves sitting right on the crest. It carried us along with it for quite a way, bubbling and boiling all around the boat, filling her up to the gunwales. Although we'd escaped speeding down the front and burying ourselves nose first at the bottom, it was still scary as we seemed to be sucked into the body of the water and became part of the wave, rather than a boat floating and bobbing on top of it. It was fast too, and we clocked over 12.5 knots, but certainly wasn't much fun.

> ⊠ *Nicky & Jan: Ladies, how fantastic is it seeing the whales. There was a tale that whales can sense when people are distressed, how good did you feel?'*

I'd been given several cards by Mum and Paul, for use on the 'down days'. So far I had avoided opening any, but that day, even though I wasn't at my lowest I felt that I had deserved the right to open one. It made me cry, but not in a sad way, more in a 'proud of who I was' kind of way. Mum had mentioned in the card how Grandma Ivy (who the boat was named after) had plenty of strength and fortitude, which helped her through life. I never got to know her well enough to realise it because she died when I was only 5 years old, but I dearly hoped I had inherited some of her resilience and that was what was helping me to carry on.

The night that followed was the worst one ever and we both definitely needed any strength and fortitude there was available. As we were settling down in the stifling heat of the cabin, Lin had the door open just a crack, with her hand on the handle ready to close it. It was something we knew we shouldn't really do, but had

155

tried it before for short periods and it gave us a little cool air in the stuffy atmosphere. Suddenly we heard the rumble of a huge wave steaming our way and Lin tried to slam the door shut, but the wave hit us a fraction of a second too soon.

It wrenched the handle out of her hand and the hatch flew open, allowing most of the wave to come in. Barbara Ivy was knocked down completely on her side and although she bounced straight back up, I ended up lying in my bed with Lin landing on top of me, and any unsecured contents of the cabin landing on top of her. At the same time the wave flooded into the cabin and topped off the pile, right in my face. I got a good idea of how a fish feels out of water – as I flapped around gasping for air, with my top half soaked.

We soon discovered there was at least an inch of water slopping around under the mattresses and everything in my corner was completely soaked. Clothes, pillows, kit in the netting (mostly water resistant thank goodness) and even Sebastian the ships' bear had a dripping paw. Our hair was sopping wet and as we took stock of the situation, we realised that it was starting to smell unpleasantly like a damp dog does!

Outside, the force of the wave had dislodged some of the dry bags, and the foot well was full of water, which meant the battery hatch would be full too unless we bailed it quickly. As I had taken the brunt of the wave inside, Lin bravely volunteered to go outside to straighten things up on deck. More waves thundered along and I could hear her sobbing outside in the pitch darkness, as I mopped up inside the cabin. We simply didn't know when the next big one might hit and I knew Lin had always been fearful about being outside at night if we capsized.

It was a horrible situation and she was extremely courageous to step so far outside her comfort zone. I was glad I wasn't out there with her, but there was still plenty to do inside to get things straight before we could rest again. I guess you know you're with the right partner when they are prepared to face their fears like that for you and I was incredibly grateful to Lin that night.

Once we were a bit more organised, we locked ourselves inside properly and kept the door firmly shut for the rest of the night. We both had wet hair and my pillows and jacket were soaked. I even got out the one dry towel that we had left, stashed away in a dry bag. It was mostly for us to use to dry ourselves, but I also wrapped it round a pillow to sleep on. It was a terrible night and we could hear the ocean crashing around relentlessly outside. We didn't get much sleep.

☒ *Jan - Lin's Mum: I hope you're both OK and that your foot isn't too painful Lin? You'll soon be able to rest and heal foot and bums! You did 49 yesterday, well done Mum xx*

It stayed rough into Day 70 (9ᵗʰ February) and we phoned Tony early on to tell him we were a bit nervous, only to find out that there wasn't likely to be any change for at least 48 hours. Apparently these were 'classic trade conditions'. We weren't impressed – classic they might be, but we didn't like them at all! We also came out in the morning to find a ship just 2 miles away; it must have passed us within half a mile but we hadn't even seen it and really didn't care right then.

But the ocean wasn't finished with us yet and though we didn't know it then, there was far worse to come later that day. Around lunchtime, Lin came out on deck to boil the kettle for our meals while I was rowing, and heading North of course. We'd been trying to dry out the cabin after our damp night, so had the mattresses up and the door open just a crack to let some air in. As we chatted, I looked over the stern of the boat and suddenly saw a huge wave building up behind us and looking particularly threatening. I managed to shout a warning to Lin just in time. Luckily she whipped round and shut the door tight. If she hadn't, there could have been a whole different ending to this story.

When the wave hit, it all happened really quickly and to be honest we'd both just expected yet another salty soaking. The wave broke over the starboard side and although we felt the boat slide sideways just as she's designed to do, the force was too much and we went over. I remember being in the water and wrenching my foot out of the steering shoe, then seeing bubbles and following them up to the surface. Lin just kept telling herself to hang on tight to the oars fastened down the sides of the boat, until she found herself in the open air again.

We came up next to each other on the starboard side, in the water, and quickly established that there were no broken bones, head injuries or limbs missing! We were stunned and shocked, yet started laughing as we tried to work out what had happened. The boat was full up with water and lying low and I grabbed a stray dry bag as it bobbed around, throwing it back into the boat, while Lin rescued her Cod & Potato dinner as it floated by – you sometimes have to get your priorities right after all! Then I got myself up into the boat and helped Lin untangle herself from the water tanks so she could get in too.

We seemed to go straight into automatic pilot and quickly listed what we'd lost overboard – incredibly only 5 things – Lin's left hand glove, my sunglasses, the compass, my drinks bottle and the broken toilet lid! We had spares of 4 of these things, and then remembered that Kakadu had sent one of my left hand gloves in the wrong size... which happened to be Lin's size! I had yet to use my last new pair, so that problem was solved and I handed over a glove.

It might sound as though we weren't affected by the capsize too much straight away, but we knew we were in shock and despite our practical nature taking control, we both knew the reaction would come later on. In our coaching sessions we'd talked about how we both react to emergency situations in a very similar way and even that raised a laugh as we joked about knowing what emotions we would have to get through over the next few hours.

The reality wasn't that funny though, and we really were on our own, 300 miles from the nearest land and in a pretty sticky situation. There simply wasn't any one around to help us and now we had to make our own decisions and control the situation as best we could. We'd already decided that we didn't want to be rescued before making our call to Tony at HQ and after speaking to him, we decided not to tell our families or mention the incident in our blog. It wouldn't have been fair to do that to them. We didn't want to worry them unnecessarily as their excitement about meeting us in Antigua was building up and were so close to the finish now it just wasn't worth it. We knew that we were OK and the boat was OK. Now we just had to get to Antigua.

☒ *Gordon: 297nm to go at 2pm today. So proud of both of you I think I'm gonna burst! You will soon be there. Just a matter of days. Luv n hugs. G&D.*

That afternoon we both had a cry as the emotion of the situation took over – just as we knew it would. I even opened Paul's special card, which was labelled '999 – for use in an emergency'. It started by saying that if I was reading the words he'd written, then it must be a really bad day and proved to be the prompt I needed to have a bit of a blub and made me feel so much better. For the rest of the day, whoever was resting stayed out on deck with the rower to show support by just being there and we decided to go onto sea anchor overnight to give ourselves chance to regroup.

> ⊠ *Caroline (ABSAR): Hope you two are OK? 297 to go, keep the pace up girls, you'll be here next weekend for that drink! Hope waves and wind behaving – still gusty here. Thinking of you. C xxx*

We wondered how Caroline seemed to know!

Chapter 17

It's hard to describe how we felt that night. Some may think it odd that the overwhelming emotion was that of calmness as we chatted through the day's events and enjoyed our favourite food and '300 miles to go' champagne that we'd missed out on at lunchtime!

I guess we knew deep down that we'd faced our biggest fear and had survived. Yet we understood that survival wasn't purely down to us. Call it luck, destiny, karma, guardian angels, whatever – but we had come out of a potential disaster virtually unscathed. There had been tears from both of us as we coped with the shock, but by evening, when the adrenaline had subsided, we felt peaceful and safe in the cabin.

We knew that we were the only boat to have capsized and it wasn't something we were proud of. So we dearly hoped the boys who had crossed the ocean in her before wouldn't think any the less of us. Lin and I both firmly believe that everything happens for a reason, and even if you don't understand the reason at the time, it will become clear eventually. Yet we really struggled to understand why it had happened to us and no one else, especially as we had been one of the best prepared teams on the water. There was no real explanation and we could only laugh about it and joke that it would make for a better story to tell when we got home.

We talked about our decision not to mention it to anyone other than the race organisers, but realised what a strain this would be. We still had several phone calls to make to family members before we arrived in Antigua and knew it would be tough to get through each one. We hoped that we would be able to keep our voices and emotions steady enough during those calls and not let on how bad things were.

Eventually we decided to email Debra and tell her about it. We figured she was probably the only person in the world who would really understand how it was for us right then. Although Debra hadn't capsized during her row, she knew us and the ocean well enough to help. There was no doubt in our minds that Debra would know exactly what to say.

We were right. As soon as she'd received our email, the texts started flooding in; a series of messages that boosted our spirits and resolve immediately, reassuring us that if we needed to talk at any time, day or night, she was there for us. It was good to know. She also emailed;

From: Debra Searle
Sent: 10th February 2008 00:27
To: Lin & Rachel at sea
Subject: Your movie doesn't end this way!

Hey Brave Ladies,
This is one of those moments when you really need to be kind to yourselves. You are so right to get the para anchor out and take some time to re-stock. This is one of those major life-changing moments that you were always going to have on this journey but they can't just be shrugged off.
Take the time to work this through in your heads and try to enjoy being grateful that you are alive and still have each other. If things get really desperate then remember that you always have that one crucial thing to turn to... laughter.
Sometimes when you have no reserves left and everything is desperate you just have to laugh at how ridiculous the situation is that you are in!
This is not how your movie is meant to end. When I run that arrival movie in my head of you rowing into English Harbour I see your Mum's both in tears - so so proud of you both and hardly able to contain their joy at your safe return. Paul and Charles are looking incredibly happy and with slight glints in their eyes as they check out your brown, toned bodies! Those first hugs with them will make all of this bad patch melt away and you won't even remember how bad it got. Liam is super proud of his Mum and thinks she is the coolest Mum in the world. Your friends and family are all cheering like crazy and are ready to party the night away with you.
Every sip of cool, cold water/beer/wine will be a taste explosion unlike anything you have experienced before and the novelty of flushing the loo will take weeks to wear off! You have so so much to look forward to. The best is yet to come. Start running your personal arrival movies in your heads - see it, smell it, taste it because that is the moment that will make all of this worth it. You have come too far to let this get you down. It can make you stronger. The choice is yours.
I am praying for you and will send texts as well, just in case this does not make it. Stay strong.
Debra
P.S. They don't need to know. Some things are better left unsaid about this journey.

That email said it all. We had come too far to contemplate any other outcome than the one we had dreamed of. We were such a strong partnership and this was our chance to show it to the world. Debra's message confirmed what we knew in our hearts – that it really was Antigua or bust!

Putting out the sea anchor that night slowed down our westerly progress, but also meant that we didn't lose too much ground, only one mile South. We pulled in the anchor tentatively the next morning and started rowing very cautiously, but our confidence was coming back stroke by stroke.

I did have some feelings of guilt to cope with because the capsize had happened while I was rowing. On my watch, if you like. I worried about whether there was something else that I should have or could have done to stop it happening, or if I had somehow caused it.

I confided in Lin about my feelings and she soon put my mind at rest. It could have happened to either of us. It was simply a freak wave that broke at the wrong time and we happened to have been in the way. That's the ocean for you; bloody Neptune and his sense of humour. We were both OK and it could have been Lin rowing when it hit – it just happened to be me. As she pointed out, it had been her who let go of the door the night before when the wave came in the cabin, and again, that could have been either of us. In fact, if it hadn't been for my warning and her quick reactions to shut the cabin hatch in time, capsizing could have been a whole different story. Lin's support meant the world to me and I felt so much better after we'd talked it through. More than ever I realised why we made such a great team.

We naturally slipped into a routine of supporting each other, with the resting person sitting outside with the rower when they could, rather than staying indoors. The water was still rough and we were distinctly more nervous than normal. But we focused on getting to Antigua and talked about what our arrival would be like. We played our favourite game of 'what will our first meal be?' and dreamed about lying in the sun by the pool at our 'Villa with a Pool'! We aimed to be there in 6 days and committed to putting all our energy into making this our last week at sea, starting with this, our final Sunday of rowing.

We did have a bit of excitement that day when I spotted a huge fish behind and under the boat. It stayed with us for a while and was about 4-5 feet long, dark coloured with big fins. At first we thought it might have been a shark, but as it swam up alongside us we spotted its long nose. It was a huge Blue Marlin! Our favourite haunt in La Gomera had been the Blue Marlin bar, so we took this to be a good omen.

I had to speak to Mum on the phone that night and it was difficult to make it through the call. She knew that I was feeling really low and was naturally concerned, but I managed not to mention what had happened and she stayed none the wiser. She was so excited about flying out to the Caribbean to meet us and happily batted away my worries about her managing to get my, Lin's and her own suitcase out there all at the same time on her own. I just couldn't wait to see her again.

We decided to metaphorically 'get back on our horse' and rowed through the night, with regular rain squalls keeping us on our toes. Thankfully it was a bit calmer, but there were some distinctly jumpy 'wide-eyed' moments and absolutely no danger of us falling asleep at the oars on that night!

⊠ *Debra Searle: The bastard of a journey really does keep testing you to the end. I had some of my hardest times in my last week! So pleased to hear progress has been good. DS.*

We took some Lucozade Recovery after the capsize to try and help our aches and pains, but unusually it reacted badly with our stomachs – which proved to be a great source of amusement as either one of us bolted out of the cabin to the loo bucket! The desalinated water we had to drink tasted so disgusting that we'd never used the tea and coffee we'd brought, instead preferring to gulp it down neat. It had a strange smooth texture to it too; almost like milk, but with a revolting taste. In that last week I found that I developed a huge thirst and craved the Lucozade (despite the side effects), or even just nice water, like it was the last drink on earth. I just couldn't wait to drink cool, clean, fresh water and begged Lin to let me crack open another ballast bottle! Of course, she wouldn't cave in to the pressure and I had to make do with yukky water for a few more days.

⊠ *George Simpson: Dr Laser Beam – Alright ladies! Well your laptop might be working but your tracker isn't and therefore all bets [for a meal at Claridges] are off! How you guys doing?*

We managed to make enough water to preen a bit and happily shaved off our Captain Caveman coverings using a mere cupful of water and some pretty heavy duty razors! We were starting to move back to civilization at last! Then as if to keep us well grounded, the beacon conked out again, and this time we had to dismantle it completely, unscrewing it and taking it right off the gunwale, switching it on and off while recording the sequence its little lights blinked at us, then fixing it back loosely. It seemed to be working again afterwards, but it was a pain to sort out because Lin had to stop rowing so I could reach under the gunwale upside down, leaning backwards limbo-fashion over the life raft in order to unscrew it – which was really tricky on a moving boat. I threatened to feed it to the sharks! Blooming useless piece of trash.

Lin also spoke to Tony to confirm that we'd made it through the night without any further excitement. Apparently he offered again to put a full maritime rescue into action, but Lin knew it was out of the question and didn't need to mention it to me – we were just so close now and simply weren't prepared to give up. So she said thanks, but no thanks.

⊠ *Russell Stynes: Rachel Lin you are awesome. So much strength, so proud to know you. Nearly there.*
Love ya, Russ.

By Day 73 (12th February), the conditions were back to their old tricks and I had a very scary and tearful moment when a huge one came over the side and we tipped up 90 degrees in a knockdown. For a split second I thought we might go right over again – and I sat on the rowing seat crying my eyes out and shaking from head to toe. When I thought about it, I wasn't actually that scared of ending up in the water again, and capsizing had been so quick we barely knew what had happened. But I knew deep down how lucky we'd been. If it happened a second or third time, the chances were that we wouldn't come out of it quite so well and that risk didn't bear thinking about.

We now had less than 200 miles to go and to be honest the finish line couldn't have come quickly enough. We were both feeling very emotional, although I knew that Lin was doing much better than me right then. In fact, on one of my more miserable days, she had a few stern words and pointed out that my mood was affecting her and bringing her down too!

It did work, but I thought how ironic it was after Lin's many down days at sea. I rather ungraciously snapped back that it was like a reverse of New Year when she'd been at her lowest and I'd had to cope with it. But it was the reminder I needed and after my next break I felt much better. I don't think until that point Lin understood the strain that her moods had been on me, but I knew that her injury had a big part to play in her overall outlook. If it had been the other way round and I'd been injured instead, I'm not sure that I could have coped with it as well as she did.

Still, it brought home to me how much your own attitude and state of mind can affect others and that it's a real responsibility you have to those around you. Allowing yourself to slide into a bad mood could be considered a kind of self-indulgent luxury, but you should be aware that there may be a price to pay when others are affected. I decided to take my own mood under better control and try my hardest to enjoy the last few days.

Mum emailed all the details over for the 'Villa with a Pool' and that certainly went some way to improving my mood - it sounded like a dream place to stay and enjoy some time in Antigua. We got on the phone to Elin and Herdip straight away to plan a party with them and any other rowers left in Antigua by the time we arrived. We just had to get through the next few days of our endurance test first.

There were lots of messages telling us to 'enjoy the last few days, you'll miss it when it's over' and much as we loved the support, we found it incredibly frustrating because it just wasn't really possible to enjoy the horrendous conditions and our well meaning supporters still had no idea how bad it had really been that week. But I really wanted to enjoy it and knew that I'd be sad as the adventure drew to a close.

⊠ *Gordon: Hi Both. Sounds like you are gonna be busy in Antigua. Don't forget to leave time to get us some Duty Free! Thinking of you every mile G&D.*

We'd been worried about the conditions that night as the forecast wasn't brilliant and although started well, by 6am it was awful. I got soaked time and time again and actually ended up sobbing at the oars. So much so that Lin came out and suggested that we tie off and let the boat drift. It's hard to believe looking back that it was so thoroughly miserable being out there right then and it wasn't even so much scary as just wet and sore.

With 155 miles to go we found ourselves working our way North once more! We were both longing to see our families and homes again and do normal things again. We knew that the last couple of days were going to be tough – we joked that Neptune must have liked us a bit too much and wasn't willing to let us go without a fight.

By Valentines Day (Day 75) we did get a bit of a break as the wind dropped and, bar one 20 minute rain storm that I got stuck in, it stayed clear for most of the night. But Lin was in a lot of pain and had to stop rowing, so we tied off at 7am for a few hours sleep. She was so determined to get there and I was in awe of her determination.

    ▪ *Emma Finn: You're nearly into single figures now.*
A strange thing to say but savour every one of those
last few miles. What an achievement!! Love & hugs,
Emma x.

While we rested we actually drifted North for once and later that day broke the magical 100 miles to go barrier, which was a cause for big celebrations and our final quarter bottle of champagne. Later on, I spoke to Paul in our weekly call and still managed not to let on what had happened, although he knew that I was finding it really hard now.

The better conditions we'd been enjoying inevitably deteriorated through the night! As I tried to get ready for my second night time rowing session, I felt 3 big hits from waves colliding with the back of the boat, which meant that I got thrown around quite a bit inside the cabin. I stuck my head out and suggested that if it was getting too rough, we tie off and rest, but Lin was adamant that it had been OK up until then and the sudden bashing was just due to three freaky waves.

By the time I came out to row a few minutes later, conditions were much worse. The boat was all over the place and Lin was in so much pain she just threw the oars down and abandoned rowing while we were sideways on. Once I'd got everything straight again it wasn't too bad; that is until the next squall started in earnest. I thought it would blow through as they normally did and opted to leave Lin undisturbed in the cabin, but after 45 minutes of constant rain I gave up. It was so windy that the stinging rain and spray from the waves was driving sideways into my eyes, and despite having my jacket fastened up and hood pulled right down, I couldn't see at all. Eventually it soaked through all the layers of my jacket leaving me dripping and despondent. I felt really awful about giving up and disturbing Lin, but it was just too much to take.

I tied off around 2am, and due to the strong NE/ENE wind

and the big swell that it created, we drifted straight back down to N16.55 degrees. AGAIN! Not only were we at the end of our tether, we were quite concerned as we now had so little time to get ourselves north again. Missing Antigua completely just wasn't an option we wanted to even consider, but right then it was starting to look like a distinct possibility!

⊠ Keith Robbins: Less than 100 miles – well done.
What on earth are you going to do once you finish?
Normal life will seem so boring. Best wishes, Keith.

But it still wasn't over and just adding to our frustration and desperation on that last full day at sea, we broke our starboard rowing gate beyond repair. It was possibly due to damage from the capsize, or from bracing the oars against the waves when it was choppy and Barbara Ivy was 'weebling' around, but either way it had cracked right through at the hinge point and couldn't be used. Luckily that meant we just had to replace the post and gate as a single unit and we managed to make the repair without losing any tools over the side. It was a slick and quick exercise; an incredible feat of skill, teamwork, surgical precision and sheer bloody mindedness, completed in near record time! Formula One car tyre changing teams would have watched in amazement at our gate changing that day!

⊠ Joe & Andrew JW: Excellent stuff girls, can't wait
for you to finish & enjoy Antigua, you will love it.
Good luck & see you in England. Andrew & Joe xx.

Later on I reorganised the wretched 36 kilo life raft, moving it from its central position and squeezing it back under the gunwale, ready to fix up the stern rowing position so that both of us could row. We thought we might have to start rowing two up earlier than we'd expected to, as it seemed we wouldn't be getting any weather assistance to help us into Antigua and we wanted to be prepared for a last dash North. It took me about 40 minutes to complete the job, but the raft did eventually squash back under the gunwale with less trouble than I was expecting. Of course, an hour later we had a text from Tony to say that the tracking beacon had packed up again and please could we fiddle with the fuse? The answer was a polite but firm 'no'! The beacon was now under the life raft and we had no intention of moving it again, so instead we compromised and promised to text our position to him every couple of hours.

⊠ Mark Heffer: Only a couple of days to go… Enjoy
the moment, it is all worth it. Mark – Mission Atlantic.

Not long after the life raft removal work, Lin had a big scare of her own with a knock down, a bit like the experience I'd had a few days before. I was getting ready to come out of the cabin and take over when a monster wave hit us hard and we turned over 90 degrees again. Lin came off the seat, which is always painful, but more so due to her injured foot. She was really shaken up and for a short time convinced herself that the ocean really was trying to kill us. I was luckier and from the relative safety of the cabin it hadn't seemed as bad for me. Lin's fear focused itself on the uneven weight distribution possibly leading to another capsize now that the life raft had been moved back to the down wind (port) side of the boat. It wasn't really logical, as the life raft had been in that position for a few weeks right at the beginning of our journey without any problems. But right then our nasty experiences were beginning to make us both look at things differently and neither of us relished the thought of another loop the loop.

When I went outside to take over rowing I moved as much equipment as I could over to the starboard side and fixed it there to help counterbalance the weight of the raft. We also agreed that if we were in the cabin resting, we would sit and sleep on the starboard side too. It did help to alleviate Lin's worry but I could see that she was still upset by what had happened.

So, I started to remind Lin about all the positive things she'd said to motivate me, even as recently as that morning, as I attempted to help lift her spirits. Sometimes it's easier to help others than it is to apply the same principles to your own situation and Lin is a great example of someone who is always there for her friends, but who sometimes neglects her own needs. Eventually she asked me to stop talking because she needed a bit time alone – but she knew that everything I'd said was true. After her next break she'd recovered well, but it just shows how much the capsize had affected us both deep down and made us behave quite out of character. We were clearly still very jumpy.

⊠ *Mandy Howlett: Mandy here, you are so nearly there, well done, keep going, thinking of you every day, hugs and kisses xxx.*

Still, getting closer to civilisation had its bonuses and we spoke to a nice, if very incredulous, Norwegian chap on a ship called Athos that passed close by. The waves were still so high that we could only see the massive ship for a couple of seconds when we were lifted up on the crests. It was completely invisible when we were in the troughs and took us a while to check that we weren't on a collision course. As the Norwegian guy glimpsed a pink flash of rowing boat through the waves, he really couldn't believe what we were doing, but he wished us well for the remainder of our journey!

⊠ *Team Cottle: Do you know your bums look big in that boat :o)*

Chapter 18

We were incredibly excited as we rowed on into what we hoped and prayed would be our last night on the water. Yet it was tinged with a bittersweet sadness because we knew that our time at sea in our little pink rowing boat was finally coming to an end.

☒ *Caroline (ABSAR): C'mon girls, big last effort and push North; know how hard you're trying, just keep at it, make it your LAST night, we're ALL waiting for you. Sending you power! C xx*

For once it was calm and clear. The stars were out in all their glory and the moon stayed up for most of the night, lighting our path across the water. We rowed right through the dark hours, travelling from 55 miles to go, down to 25 miles to go by daybreak. It was a fabulous night and I loved it. It felt very peaceful out there and I really enjoyed it – for me it was probably the best night of the whole crossing and everything I'd dreamed that rowing across an ocean might be. The calm conditions felt like a sign that we'd made it – we'd coped with everything Neptune and his buddies could throw at us and come out the other side where the most beautiful night was our reward. Our excitement grew when we saw planes in the sky too, it was a sure sign of civilisation as we headed towards the finish line.

☒ *Donna Malcolm: Bring forth the heroes inside you, going for the line! Pain will go away. Glory will last forever! One more stroke! D x*

The moon passed overhead and went down around 2.30am. But it took another hour for me to realise that the glow on the horizon that I could see over my left shoulder wasn't the remains of the moon light... it was Antigua! I ummed and ahhd about whether to wake Lin up to see it straightaway, but there was only about half an hour to go until she came out to row, so I decided to contain my euphoria and let her sleep on.

When she came out around 4am, I was literally bursting with excitement but took a deep breath and whispered to her to look over my shoulder and tell me what she could see. At first, as she gazed towards the horizon, she couldn't believe it and was convinced it was just the glow from the setting moon. Then, when

I told her the moon had gone down ages ago, we both cheered and leapt (as much as was possible on our dodgy pins) around the deck a bit! We could even see the flashing lights on the radio masts, and the glow from Guadeloupe over our right shoulders. We had just a few miles to go, with the great conditions we were exactly in the position we wanted to be in, and now the end was actually in sight.

> ⊠ *Nicky, Trina & Patrick: Oh my God you've only gone & done it. How proud are we. You made me cry, I am so happy you are coming home Lin, I've missed you. Love you lots xxxx*

At the next handover, I was slowly waking up inside the cabin when I realised that I could hear Lin talking to herself. At first I thought she might be singing away, and I smiled to myself, but then the tone of voice changed to become more and more desperate. I couldn't work out why that would be the case, because we were getting one of the smoothest nights ever across the waves. Then I heard her making a weird swooshing noise. I stuck my head out of the cabin to see what on earth was happening, only to find Lin waving a rope around her head like a lasso and 'shooeing' at something in the darkness.

Apparently a crazy bird had flown over to have a look at the boat, but kept flying a bit too close for comfort, right in Lin's face. It got so near to her that she could actually see its beady eye glinting in the darkness. She kept trying to shout quietly to scare it away without waking me up, but it wouldn't leave, so in the end she resorted to waving the rope around to discourage it! It was just so funny to be buzzed by a bird on that last night and we were thankful it hadn't landed in our lap as happened to on of the guys on No Fear! I kept the rope handy for my shift and the bird did come back, but it never got that close again thank goodness.

When daylight broke, the island disappeared from sight. But conditions stayed good and we couldn't have been more upbeat and excited that day. Whoever was resting continually strained their eyes towards the West, longing for the magical moment when we'd see Antigua on the horizon. We were literally aching for a glimpse of land and couldn't believe it was nearly 11 weeks since we'd last seen any. We posted our final 'land ahoy' blog and a photograph on the website, together with a cryptic message to let readers know that there was something important we hadn't yet told them about our crossing. We suggested they kept reading the blog once we'd landed and promised to spill the beans as soon as we could – but of course we needed to tell our families first. Honesty had always been our policy with our supporters and as easy as it would have been (and far less embarrassing) we weren't going to start covering up things like a capsize now!

Land Ahoy!

☒ *Christina Jenkins – Breast Cancer Care: This is it. Last few hours, Take it all in & treasure it. Words don't describe my admiration for you both. You've conquered your dreams. LOL xx*

Our instructions were to radio in to Antigua and Barbuda Search and Rescue (ABSAR) when we were 20 miles out from the island. ABSAR support the race from Antigua and send out a boat to escort the rowers across the finish line and record your official finish time. We duly made our radio call and the lovely, smooth American accent of Jonathan Cornelius acknowledged. He asked us to call again at 10 miles out and said he would see us soon. By now we were weak-kneed with excitement, partly because we were now so close but mostly due to Jonathan's marvellous voice.

Then suddenly, out of the haze on the horizon, we made out the dark smudge of Antigua topped by fluffy white clouds. We were ecstatic, and while still mindful of the conditions and their ability to change rapidly, we knew without any doubt at that point that we really would make it all the way – from land to land across the Atlantic Ocean in a rowing boat!

☒ *Joe Cottle: To Rachel, well done and will U marry me. Joe (Syd's nephew). PS. I am only 12.*

⊠ *Joe Cottle: Lin, in case Rachel says No, will you marry me instead?*

The afternoon was incredibly hot and sunny so we decided to wash our hair one last time in an effort not to repel our much loved family and friends by our stinkyness when we landed. We had music playing out on deck and the sea stilled to the calmest we had ever seen it. It was glassy and slick, sparkling in the baking hot sunshine. Life seemed pretty good as Lin primped and preened, getting ready for our big moment. We even hoped we might get a last visit from some dolphins, but I guess they had other things to do and weren't coming out to play that day!

Just as I was getting to the end of my shift and dreaming of my hair wash, the sky suddenly clouded over and Lin was kind enough to take over the oars early so that I could wash my hair before it rained. We knew by then that we were likely to arrive in the early evening local time, and although it would be dark, we wanted to look our best and try not to smell too much for those first, much dreamed of hugs with our families. After a lovely sponge down wash, we also donned our special 'coming home' outfits – a set of clean and dry clothes that we'd fanatically protected in dry bags from day one. Plus, we got out the extra special, cream, fluffy sheepskin seat covers, similarly cosseted all the way across the ocean just for this moment.

⊠ *Caroline (ABSAR): You're doing it. Fantastic effort Pink Ladies. Monitoring VHF – heard you this am – call us at 10 miles out. Can't WAIT to see you out there. I'll need tissues!!*

First sight of Antigua under the clouds

We also had a funny incident when a small boat chugged past during the afternoon. I was rowing along happily and could hear the motor for a while before I saw anything, which was a little scary, as I didn't recognise the noise at all and couldn't work out what it was. I guess I just hadn't heard anything like an engine for so long. Eventually, I could see something that looked strangely familiar, yet really out of place, bobbing across the waves less than half a mile away. I just couldn't place it at all and racked my brain to work out what it looked like. Then it hit me... a sofa! From this angle the little boat looked just like a lovely upholstered sofa with big comfortable arms!! I knew right there and then that I'd been at sea for far too long! Lin couldn't stop laughing at me!

⊠ *Ned Skelton: Dear R&L, hydrate well because you will lose a litre in tears if I know anything at all. I am so proud knowing you two. I am thinking of you. Ned & co.*

The next handover was just before the 10 miles to go call, so Lin got to speak with Jonathan of the fabulous voice. Next she set up the stern footplate, and after a short rest joined me on the oars – just as the sky misted over and the mother of all rainstorms started. So much for our clean, dry shorts and the gorgeous, fluffy seat covers that we'd kept pristine for our arrival!

It rained so hard that we couldn't actually see anything, and Antigua disappeared into the mist in a highly disconcerting fashion. I mean, that land stuff is pretty solid and shouldn't just evaporate... or had it all been a mirage after all?! Not being able to see anything but the next wave, we had to rely purely on the GPS that we'd brought out on deck to guide us, as we wriggled back into our big jackets and tried in vain to keep our freshly washed hair dry under the hoods.

But nothing was going to get us down for long that day, and we sang along happily to the music as we rowed ever closer. I should point out that neither of us can actually sing (although we sang a lot on the way across) but we're as bad as each other and it didn't matter as we plodded on towards where we'd last seen Antigua! We stopped every mile or two for water and so that Lin could stretch out her painful feet. Soon, it was time for our final call to ABSAR – 5 miles to go and Jonathan's assurance that he'd be seeing us very soon!

A couple of miles later and suddenly the cloud and mist lifted. As I turned around, I could see the incredible sight of cliffs, buildings and waves breaking on a beach – Antigua was back and very, very real! I squawked in surprise and as our oars clashed together, Lin turned round to see what had made me stop rowing. Then she squeaked in surprise too. It was quite scary to see land so near to us and we could actually hear the waves breaking which was pretty much terrifying. It actually made us want to row away so we didn't get too close, but we knew that we needed to be within a mile of Cape Shirley, whichever bit of land that was, in order to make the finish line and claim our race position.

As dusk settled we rowed nearer, deciding to go against our instinct to run away, and instead tuck in as close as we dared because we knew there was a sharp turn into English Harbour right after the finish line. But as a final reminder of who's really in charge out there on the water, we got caught by the wind on our approach to the island and blown quickly to about half a mile South of where we wanted to be. Yet again, and right to the line, we had a battle to go North once again. It may have seemed ironic but our frustration levels were off the scale as we fought and clawed our way back to where we wanted to be.

Eventually, as we rowed into the lee of the island, we got a good line and moved in close to shore. Although I'd spent hours studying the chart, we weren't entirely sure which bit of headland we were actually aiming for and we couldn't see Cape Shirley Lighthouse anywhere. The noise of the waves crashing on the rocks was filling our ears and scaring us; we just hadn't heard anything like it for such a long time. Then, our senses went into complete overdrive as we got close enough to smell the land – the intense scent of wet, tropical rain forest! A little further on though and as we were rowing past Eric Clapton's house Lin became convinced she could smell bacon frying. It was definitely time for us to finish!

The storm clouds that had brought all the rain earlier moved away to the South of us, towering up and billowing high into the sky, lit majestically with deep shades of orange, pink and purple by the setting sun. Of all the sunsets we had seen, this was by far the best, and it seemed like a truly spectacular and fitting final curtain to our journey.

As darkness descended, we switched on the Nav light, keeping a keen ear open for the sound of the ABSAR boat coming to meet us and escort us across the finish line. We did hear a couple of engines and got quite excited, but they proved to be light aircraft rather than a RIB, so with just 1.5 miles to the finish, I commented to Lin that if the ABSAR boat hadn't arrived in another half mile, then I would radio again. We really didn't want to miss them or the finish!

No sooner had I spoken than with a crash and a roar, out of nowhere, a huge RIB rocketed out of the darkness at high speed! We jumped out of our skins – it scared the bejeebers out of us! We immediately recognised Amanda from the race organisers onboard, and Caroline, who had sent such wonderful messages from Antigua in the last few weeks was right by her side. Everyone onboard the RIB was whooping and cheering and as they circled round us, they introduced us to a special visitor they had on board.

Lin's son Liam was duly prodded unwillingly to the front of the RIB at which point Lin couldn't contain it any longer and burst into tears at the sight of 'her boy'. Of course this set me off, and then all the girls on the ABSAR boat joined in too! Liam, being a teenager, appeared mortified at the sight of the blubbing women and quite disturbed that his cool was being so badly compromised. But he quickly re-established his street cred with some typically monosyllabic teenage answers to his Mum's questions!

Final approach to English Harbour

Jonathan, owner of the lovely American voice, was driving and told us to head for a big chunk of land, which apparently was the finish line. I asked how close in to the headland we could get and he reassured me that we could get very close without being smashed onto the rocks. As he's the person in charge of rescues, I figured he knew what he was talking about, so we set our course for Cape Shirley. We only found out later that the lighthouse that we'd been looking for, which is marked on the chart, actually fell down years ago!

When Jonathan challenged us to sprint the last 500m to the finish, we decided we should show him and the rest of the team how it's done! As Lin said, there's life in the old pair yet. So to a call of two, one, reach; we stretched out together, rose to the challenge and pushed a bit harder, in perfect unison and smooth as you like, hitting 4 knots over the line, to the sound of cheers and hooters. It was an amazing finish to our race. It had taken us 76 days, 11 hours and 12 minutes.

As we slowed down and followed the RIB round the headland and into English Harbour we thought we could see and smell something industrial and crinkled our noses up at the acrid, oily smell. We found out later that the lights and smell that we thought was some kind of oil terminal, was actually from the masts and diesel engines of the luxury and very expensive boats in Falmouth Harbour next door! Our over sensitive noses were obviously playing tricks on us already.

As we carefully navigated round the rocks and into the channel, we were taken by surprise as flares went off, high up on the old Fort at the entrance to English Harbour, lighting our way with a bright red glow and serving as an early warning to supporters that we were on our way in. A photographer buzzed around us in a dinghy, snapping pictures of our bemused faces, while I was trying to avoid hitting any of the boats moored up and still keep the ABSAR RIB in sight so we knew where to go.

Rowing past the Fort – Gordon and Dave lighting the way

177

As we carried on, half laughing and half crying, we were completely and utterly overwhelmed. People came out on the decks of their boats and cheered. Horns were going off everywhere and we had to answer dozens of questions, shouted to us across the water from all directions. We rowed past a waterside bar and everyone came out to watch us go by; then when they realised we were a women's team, they went completely mental, shouting and cheering and setting off a raft of new emotions for us.

Eventually, the RIB moved away to moor up in a different part of the harbour, and I could just about make out the quayside, with a neat little Barbara Ivy sized space at the end. We'd hoped for about 20 people to welcome us in, but this was a Saturday night and the local bars and restaurants had emptied as people wanted to see us arrive. There were what seemed like hundreds of figures standing and watching, and seeing so many faces was actually quite scary in a way. Suddenly it seemed very important that we came in to moor up correctly and finish off the race in the same professional way that we had aimed to do everything – we felt that we owed it to Barbara Ivy. As we inched closer, we realised how big the crowd really was as yet more flares and horns went off. It was amazing, unbelievable and fantastic.

At last we were there, and our emotions were all over the place as we glided in perfectly alongside the quay. We could see so many people, but couldn't quite make out faces in the bright lights, and with the tears in our eyes. Then Lin shouted out;

'Rach, you'll never guess who I've just seen, it's your brother'. I looked up and there he was, standing next to Mum, with Dave just behind. He'd flown out to Antigua to surprise me, and boy, was it a surprise. I never expected to see him there, tears pouring down his face, the proudest a brother could be. It had been him up on the Fort, lighting the sky with flares to welcome us in and he'd completely fooled us with the text message the day before asking for us to take some duty free home for him. He'd sent that message while sitting in the sun right there in English Harbour! Then I noticed Anne and Robert (my aunt and uncle) over to the edge of the crowd, while John (Lin's dad) and Liam were at the front on the quayside.

We shipped the oars as Amanda and the ABSAR team arrived across the grass to secure the boat for us. I felt a pang of sadness as I realised that our life onboard Barbara Ivy was nearly over and we had to share her now. Part of me still didn't want to get off at all. We took our big jackets off and put on our clean dry t-shirts again. As we lit our own flares to celebrate our achievement, we spontaneously reached out to hold hands in celebration – we'd only gone and bloomin' done it!

Champagne celebrations with the Ready, Steady, Cook bottle

Amanda opened a bottle of champagne over us, but we parried back with the Ready Steady Cook bottle, complete with the red and green ribbons, that we'd carried safely all the way from the UK. Lin let rip with it all over me and the crowd, but there was plenty left for us to drink too. Eventually though, the time had come and although we'd subconsciously delayed it, we really did have to get off the boat. It was an emotional moment as we looked up at the waiting, expectant crowd.

We turned to look at each other and reached out to hold hands again. Then, just as we'd always planned we made that monumental step off the boat, still best friends, at exactly the same time – the 43rd and 44th women to row any ocean. It was an awesome moment. Amanda reached down for me on one side and John grabbed Lin from the other and if they hadn't, we would certainly have fallen over – as that dry land stuff proved to be quite tricky straight away! They had to hold us up for a while before we could stand unaided. After 11 weeks at sea, our leg muscles had wasted away and our bodies adapted to the constantly moving environment, but as we stood on shaky legs like newborn foals, our families flocked around and we felt ourselves supported as we finally enjoyed those much dreamed of hugs.

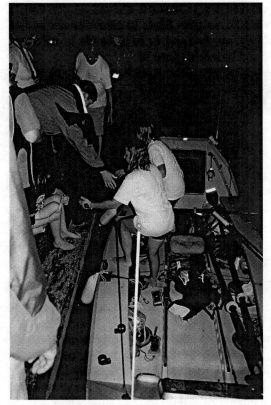

The first step onto dry land!

Time then passed in a bit of a blur. Someone gave us Breast Cancer Care t-shirts and we were shepherded and half carried to a big Breast Cancer Care banner to pose for photos. We stood propping each other up! There were balloons, pink champagne and so many congratulations from the numerous onlookers, most of who we didn't know!

At some point in the proceedings, Lin took a deep breath and started the story about the capsize. Everyone was stunned into silence for a while as they absorbed the words and then the reality of what had happened just a week before. Happily they understood why we hadn't told them about it at the time and they were amazed that we'd managed to keep it to ourselves without letting on. But more than anything now they were just relieved that we had made it across in one piece.

We also fired up the laptop in front of witnesses – to prove we'd won our bet with Dr Laser Beam (George Simpson). He bet that we couldn't get a laptop across the ocean in full working order but our trusty Panasonic Toughbook didn't let us down. We're still waiting for the meal at Claridges!

First hugs – Mum and Gordon holding me up!

Later, as the crowd filtered away, we wobbled to the ladies toilets like a pair of drunks, hanging onto any available props. It was hysterical as we focused on a point we wanted to get to, then criss-crossed our way to it. My aunt even had to rescue me from one particularly dangerous trajectory as I crabbed sideways in completely the wrong direction, down a slipway towards the water! At one point, Lin felt faint and had to lie down, much to Mum's consternation because she was lying on top of an ant's nest. Lin simply didn't care and wasn't moving anywhere! I meanwhile, was still enthusing about the 'proper' toilets, which were a far cry from our Luggable-loo! We also got to take a sip of the cold bottled water that Mum had brought for us. It was fantastic, so clean, cool and fresh. I don't think I've ever tasted anything quite so nice.

We both felt sad to leave Barbara Ivy that night. She'd done such a great job in looking after us and getting us there and she looked so peaceful moored up against the quay, gently moving with the water. Before we left for the villa we both got back on the boat (and found it far easier to balance!) to say our own personal goodbyes to her. We knew we'd see her again the next morning, but it was hard to accept that part of the adventure was over now and we had to move on, ready or not.

Eventually, the families got us a taxi and we headed up to the 'villa with a pool' where our first meal was hot buttered toast and a cup of tea! After playing with the flushing toilets and sticking our heads in the fridge (we'd missed chilled things a lot!) we got to have the best shower ever. Mum had brought out some scrubby sponges for us to use and we enjoyed scouring off the results of nearly 3 months of washing with baby wipes. The villa showers were outdoors, so my first heavenly wash was taken with tropical plants all around, and the stars twinkling and shining down through the mesh ceiling.

Sticking our heads in the fridge seemed like a good idea at the time!

Bed came next and I was tired beyond exhaustion. It was a good thing that my bed was huge too, because every time I rolled over in the night it felt as though I was going to fall out – a bit like when you've had too much to drink and the room swims around you. So I planted myself right in the middle and drifted off safe in the knowledge that I had 1.5 rolls in either direction before I hit the floor! But the bed was warm and dry, I could hear plants rustling outside and bullfrogs croaking rather than oars creaking, the sheets weren't encrusted with salt and most of all it wasn't really moving. And… I didn't have to get up in 2 hours time and go rowing again!

Chapter 19

The next morning I woke early and in my wibbly wobbly way, tiptoed out into the living room. Though the couple of small steps on the way proved to be a bit more of a challenge than I first imagined. The sun was shining through the big windows and I went outside with a glass of juice to sit and gaze across the harbour where the water glittered in the light.

⊠ *George Simpson: Welcome to the club! You rock. Well done.*

It was so strange to think that just last night we'd rowed around the headland now in front of me and into the harbour. I felt quite emotional just thinking about it, and remembering life onboard as I sat for the first time in 11 weeks on a dry seat that didn't move.

My brother came out for a swim in the pool and we sat in the peaceful morning sun together, chatting about our experiences. It had been such a surprise to see him there, but I was so pleased that he'd decided to make the journey. He told me that he'd made the decision the minute that we rowed out of La Gomera – he'd been there for the start of our adventure and he knew that he needed to be there to see us finish at the other end.

That morning I had my first bath in 11 weeks – and it was truly amazing! Although I struggled to get much water in the tub, it was a bath nonetheless and I lay there thinking about all the times onboard when I'd missed a hot bubble bath with a vengeance. I thought back to the last time I luxuriated in the tub in our hotel room in La Gomera, on the morning that we left, and it seemed like a million years ago. Getting dressed was amusing too, as none of my clothes fitted me any more. What had been snug fitting shorts in La Gomera now looked like they belonged to a giant as I slipped them on without undoing the fasteners and hoiked the waistband in with a belt. I think I'd lost about 2½ stones (35 lbs) in weight and needless to say, I quite liked the new me!

Later on we all walked slowly down to the boat, which was quite ambitious for Lin and I, and more than a little painful on our shaky legs! We were still taking a wayward route to any given point that we aimed for and had discovered a tendency to just stagger and fall over without notice when we were trying to stand still!

Barbara Ivy was there, sitting just where we'd left her, bright pink in the strong sunlight, and attracting a huge amount of attention from cruise ship visitors who had come to see Nelsons Dockyard. Getting any work done proved to be nigh on impossible as we were bombarded with congratulations and questions, and included in photos and video.

Skinny me!

🗙 *Hilary Williams: Congratulations! So pleased & so proud. Hugs from us all. Enjoy the rest & reflect on the enormity of it all! Don't forget lipstick! Hil x*
🗙 *Saltwater PR: Congratulations for reaching the finish line! Hope you're having a well deserved rest & your land sickness isn't too bad! Love Saltwater x*

But there was one really important job to do that day. Elin and Herdip, with whom we'd shared so much in the last tough weeks, were due to arrive that afternoon, hopefully after their supporters, whose flight was due to land just after lunchtime. It was going to be a close run thing as to who arrived first. Every so often we got a report of how close the girls were, and we texted them ourselves to wish them well. At last, we got the news that they had crossed the finish line – just as their families burst out of a taxi and ran across the grass, suitcases akimbo. It was incredibly emotional as Lin and I hugged them with tears in our eyes. We knew how important it had been to us to have family there to greet us and how important to the family to be there too.

Just a few minutes later, the flares went off on the fort and we picked out Dream Maker, moving slowly through the moorings. Lin and I were already in tears – our own raw emotions still running high. Eventually we couldn't contain the excitement and set off our own flares, to guide the girls in to the quayside - a bit too well as it turned out and they rammed the wall, bows on! But it was a very special moment for us when we took their lines and reached down to help them take that epic first step up onto dry land – I guess it felt a bit like it completed the circle for us.

I'll never forget how it felt to watch the scenes of joy unfold before us. Families and friends reunited, an incredible achievement by two amazing women, and the relief of having all boats across with no loss of life or serious injury. With our own arrival less than 24 hours before, it was a whirlwind of emotion as we laughed and cried along with them.

> ☒ *Team Cottle: Oi land lubbers! Where is your land-based update? We reckon you have capsized but not told anyone. I reckon it's because RQS is top heavy!*

By the next day, we'd managed to get in touch with all of our close friends and relatives to break the news about the capsize. So the time had come to 'fess up' and post our special blog on the web site. Both of us were in tears again as we relived the experience together and we wondered what the reaction would be. Would people be critical and scornful of our ability? Or think that we shouldn't have been out there in the first place? We didn't have long to wait to find out and we really shouldn't have worried.

> ☒ *Hilary Williams: Not sure if you still get these. But CONGRATULATIONS. Cried when you finally crossed line. Tears poured when read of capsize! You are OARSOME! Hil x*

We found out a couple of days later that Hilary had posted a congratulations card to us in Antigua. When we received the card a couple of days later, we noticed that very spookily it had been postmarked on the very day we capsized.

> ☒ *Emma Finn: Have just read your last two blogs with tears streaming down my face. It makes your achievement even more spectacular! You're two very tough cookies! Love Emma.*

The rest of our time in Antigua was spent on Antigua time! Slow and relaxing, eating and drinking well as our bodies started to heal and recover. Our salt sores improved rapidly in the dry conditions and it was noticeable how much our 'padding' improved from the first night that we sat (or tried to sit) uncomfortably on the wooden seats in the Mad Mongoose!

We had to get the boat ready for shipping and it took time and a strong stomach to clean her from top to toe - especially the festering bin locker! We'd saved the remains of an unlucky flying fish to show everyone what they looked like, and a tank of the dreaded 'watermaker' juice for them to try. It was the funniest thing to see them all take a gulp, faces screwed up at the taste of the vile stuff, while Gordon just spray-spat his straight back out. They couldn't believe we'd survived on it for nearly 3 months.

⊠ *Akemi & the Cottage Kids in Japan: Omedeto!*
Congratulations. Thank you for letting us know you
and meet you. We are so proud of you. Myoko (Akemi)
& Cottage Kids.

Antigua is a paradise island and I fell in love with it completely. One afternoon I walked up to the fort with Mum, Gordon and Dave, and we sat on the wall overlooking the harbour entrance. As I looked out over the brilliant blue water to the horizon, it seemed hard to believe that we'd rowed all that way and as Gordon described what they'd seen and experienced on that night we arrived, I felt very emotional. The water seemed so beautiful and serene from up there, yet I knew only too well that the ocean is a fickle beast.

We did have our barbeque at the 'Villa with a Pool' too. We invited everyone and anyone connected with the rowing race – but best of all, Elin and Herdip came along, reminding us of the friendship that built up during those desperate days at sea when we first planned our party. We cracked all the light sticks that we had onboard and dotted them around the pool as decorations, then made a huge rum punch. Titi Thwaites, our land lord came along (probably to make sure we weren't trashing the place!) and left full of beer, incredulous that such a 'little rower' could take on the Atlantic, and promising to lend us a car so that we could go sightseeing round the island.

We took him up on the offer, and toured the tourist spots, somewhat scared by travelling so fast. Even 40mph seemed frightening to us after our sedentary ocean crossing! Gordon specifically wanted to swim on both sides of the island – in the Atlantic Ocean and Caribbean Sea. So we did! I never knew my brother was such a water baby, so maybe it does run in the family. It was great to spend some quality time with him as a result of the challenge, which has inevitably brought us much closer together.

⊠ *Peter Brown: Fantastically well done girlies!! Sorry a bit belated... scary last week of the cruise!! When is the book out... TV documentary?*

I got to spend some time with Mum too and while we were out for lunch one day, I spotted a lady sitting at the bar. Her t-shirt looked familiar, and without looking like some sort of stalker, I tried to get a closer peek. Sure enough, the logo on the back included crossed over dragon boat paddles and a pink ribbon. Whoever this lady was, she had to be something to do with dragon boats and breast cancer. Plucking up all my courage I went over, introduced myself and said I'd noticed her t-shirt. Sure enough Kathie Menogue was a member of a breast cancer survivor's dragon boat racing team from Canada and had only been admiring Barbara Ivy minutes before. She was in Antigua on holiday and so thrilled to hear our story. She later left the t-shirt on the boat as a gift for me – and we've been in touch since we both got home. It's amazing how sport can so often prove to be a common denominator and make the world's boundaries even smaller.

We all made it up to Shirley Heights for the Sunday night festivities, as per our instructions from Steve and Paul on The Reason Why, and boy was it worth it. Lin and I gazed out across the sea (which again looked so calm!) from where we were, high up above the finish line, to the horizon that we'd crossed just a few days before. With tears in our eyes, we hugged as we sat on the cliff top and watched the sun go down, still barely able to comprehend our achievement.

On my last day in Antigua I took up Jonathan's offer to go out for a spin in the ABSAR boat. ABSAR is the Antiguan version of the RNLI, dedicated to helping keep people safe, run by volunteers and dependent on donations. The deal was that I had to jump in and scrape the hull, but that seemed easy peasy lemon squeesy now – compared to doing it on an ocean rowing boat mid-Atlantic! It was a lovely afternoon, spent speeding down the South coast of Antigua at a mind-blowing 30 knots. In comparison our average speed rowing across had been a mere 1.7 knots. We moored up on a buoy and donned snorkels to clean the bottom of the boat, before swimming along a reef gazing at the beautiful fish and coral. I only just had time to pack before leaving for the airport!

Yes, there was rum punch involved!

Playing on the ABSAR boat.

I felt sad to leave the island, but as ever, time moves on relentlessly and eventually we had to wake up from the dream-like tropical existence and go home. Of course the good side was that Paul was going to be there, waiting for me after so many months apart. But the bad side being that it would be cold, wet and dreary, and we'd have to get back to reality – whatever reality actually was now. I had a feeling that was going to take some figuring out.

Chapter 20

We arrived back at Heathrow to the expected cold, damp and dismal British winter morning. But things brightened up as we walked through the arrivals hall to be greeted by Jo and Lou (of fish joke fame) and Christina from Breast Cancer Care. With a big welcome home banner and bunches of flowers, we felt just a little bit special as we headed for a coffee and to record a podcast for the Breast Cancer Care website. It was great to see everyone again, lots of fun to hear their side of the story and as ever, the emotions weren't far from the surface.

It was strange to say goodbye to Lin too. The time had come for us to go our separate ways after being in each others pockets for a time far longer than the actual row. I'd become so used to us being together, I wondered how it would feel not having her nearby although I knew we probably needed some time on our own to get used to life on land. But there were more surprises too and a few hours later, as the car turned into my street, Paul was on the doorstep to welcome me home with a huge banner across the gates and a house full of balloons. At last I could have the hug that I'd been waiting for all those weeks and it was certainly worth the wait. It was fantastic to see him again and to know that despite his initial misgivings about my choice of challenge, he couldn't have been more proud of my achievement.

I had a week to spare before having to go back to work, and while driving back from a radio interview one day, I heard a song on the radio that was very close to my heart. With tears pouring down my face, I struggled to drive (I was still finding British speed limits terrifying anyway!) as my memory took me back to the amazing star-lit nights out at sea. It seemed that adjusting back to real life was going to prove tricky with emotional incidents popping up when you least expected them!

So many things seemed strange to begin with. The cold and damp, the speed of traffic, noises - like people talking and sirens, being in a crowd, watching TV, being able to eat normal food! My sense of smell had obviously changed in the clean ocean air and went into overdrive at any given opportunity, regardless of whether the scent was good or bad!

My welcome back to work was good too and everyone allowed me the time and space get used to it again. But things had changed while I was away and it was like working for a different company. The global credit problems were impacting on the Bank and we knew that there were going to be difficult times ahead. I felt quite disconnected from what was going on around me and without enough work to fill the days, started to have a long hard think about the future.

I was thoroughly enjoying the many public speaking engagements and other opportunities that the row seemed to be producing and I was quite happy to 'go with the flow' and just see where these opportunities took me. One nice surprise was to be asked to work for the Prince's Trust, initially delivering motivational speeches about the dragon boat racing and the row, but then developing into coaching and helping to deliver the program. I've met some amazing young people through this work and they never cease to inspire me.

But I missed the ocean dreadfully and still do. Throughout my time at sea I was continually fascinated by the ever-changing moods of the ocean and sky – shown in colours, shapes, sounds and movement. Driving up the motorway with Paul one clear night I ended up twisting my head round at an impossible angle, getting quite stressed just because I couldn't see the stars properly. Although I'd hated the whistling wind, I never tired of the sound of the waves and felt overwhelmed by the 'normal' noises around me. I had thrived on the space and solitude – that feeling of being a tiny speck on a huge ocean, with an endless horizon all round and I found myself gazing out of the window at work, needing space and wondering what the future held.

I needed to reflect on the whole challenge too. At the time we finished our row, 187 women had successfully summited Everest, 50 female astronauts had been into outer space, but only 46 women had ever rowed any ocean and we were the 43rd and 44th. I think that puts it well and truly into perspective. There's no question that what we achieved was huge, life-changing and spectacular and it does make others view you in a different light. But we'd learnt so much from the row about ourselves and each other. I knew that we had faced our fears head on and if not overcome them, then at least found a way to cope. We'd lived side by side in impossible conditions, yet managed not to fall out. We'd seen some amazing sights and experienced Mother Nature (or maybe our old buddy

Neptune!) at best and worst. But most of all we had laid our souls bare to the world and opened ourselves up to the worst possible outcome – that of failure. Yet we had succeeded against the odds.

We learnt more than ever to look for the positive in every situation and when things get desperate, to take control of whatever you can. Taking control of even something very small, like deciding to change the rowing shift pattern for a bit, or cleaning the cabin out, can make all the difference to how you mentally approach the bigger picture. After our endless battles North (18 different times in total) I also realised that you can only ever make a decision based on the information in front of you and once you've made it, there's no point in beating yourself up if later it turns out that a different choice may have been better. You didn't know that at the time and just need to remain flexible and react to what happens around you, while considering all the options for the future.

We both had good and bad days out there, and the challenge taught us to be more tolerant, but also more assertive. All of us are capable of so much more mental and physical challenge than we could ever imagine, if only we give ourselves a chance. We also found that we can both be far more resourceful, resilient, inventive and innovative than we first thought!

My appreciation of day-to-day things has also improved – a soft, dry and clean bed, flushing toilets, fresh food, untainted water and having Christmas dinner with my family are top of the list. I've spent a lot more time with family members since I got back too, especially my brother, and I will always be grateful for their love and support throughout the adventure.

As I look back over the years, I do sometimes wonder how many of my nine lives I've already used up with near misses or incidents that could have turned out a whole lot differently – being in freezing water for over 10 minutes after the dragon boat swamped and sank, having a horse rear up and fall over backwards on top of me, a nasty incident with a car crash in Toronto, and of course, the mid-Atlantic capsize. While it makes me wonder how many lives are left, I also remember the adventures and experiences gained alongside those incidents. And I know which way round I'd rather have it.

Although I'm fundamentally the same person, the challenge has changed me and it took a bit of time to find out exactly how. If I'm honest, I'm probably still working it out. I know I'm more confident in some ways than before, and feel far more capable of taking on whatever life decides to throw at me. I am less intimidated by others, because I know that if anyone tries to put me down now, I can always pull out my trump card of having rowed an ocean. It works every time! I also quite liked the new feeling of calmness and being at peace with myself, rather than the stress bunny I'd become at work before I left. So I've promised myself to keep finding ways to get it back if it goes away – normally a trip out on the water does the trick!

I visited Debra a few months after getting back and it was great to see her and be able to say thank you for all the support and encouragement. We certainly wouldn't have considered the challenge if it wasn't for Debra, and her support definitely made a huge difference, especially in that horrendous, desperate final week at sea. There is also a certain comfort to be gained from being around other ocean rowers – call it mutual respect, a sense of camaraderie, whatever – you know you've seen and experienced things that no one else will ever understand and that brings with it a certain connection.

I'd like to use all of this experience to get more out of life in general and will definitely be spending more time at sea in the future. In the meantime, when I'm feeling stifled by the daily grind, simply gazing at the clouds and sky (day or night) helps to conjure up the incredible memories of the space, solitude, peace and freedom of life out at sea. And of course, remembering life at sea is never better than when lying in my idea of heaven - a hot bath!

In the summer after I got back, I joined a crew to do a yacht delivery from London round the South coast to Brixham. We had to complete the delivery in 5 days and were sailing shorthanded, so with no previous experience, I was quite nervous about the trip and desperate not to let either myself or the crew down. It was hard work as the wind was against us and we ended up motoring most of the way in a reasonable swell. But I found the night shifts relatively easy, the wave size didn't bother me, I knew that I wasn't even near my physical and mental limits, didn't get sea sick and discovered that I can sleep quite happily with my head on a diesel engine!

On the last night, the other two crew members were both asleep below deck and I had a couple of hours on my own. The sun was setting in beautiful red and orange colours, silhouetting a fishing boat in the distance and there were some big birds swooping around calling to each other. The choppy sea was calming and the wind easing off a bit – leaving just me, the boat and the ocean. I felt perfectly calm, peaceful and at home on the water.

The end.

We finished the row still as best friends, just as we'd planned!

Postscript

We often get asked what we did after the row, so here's a quick summary:

Firstly, we are still best friends! We had a few months where we needed to concentrate on getting back to reality, but we are closer than ever even now. We both feel that it was very much a team effort and we know without doubt that we both had the right person on our team. I can't think of anyone who I'd rather have taken on the challenge with.

Both of us went back to our jobs and tried to settle back into 'normal' life as best we could, though we found it incredibly hard. We took up the offer of completing our Day Skipper qualifications and have had a lot of fun sailing. One day we'd love to sail together across the Atlantic and right back to English Harbour!

Lin changed her job, got married and now has an adorable baby son called Lewis, brother to Liam. She spent most of the year after the row on crutches and was eventually diagnosed with psoriatic arthritis, a horrible condition where, in simple terms, her immune system attacks itself. It is hereditary, but is believed to have been triggered by the physical stress of the row and exacerbated by injuries picked up out at sea. But Lin will tell you that even if she knew this would happen before the row, she'd still have done it. More sailing is definitely on the cards in the future.

As for me... I still live with Paul in Chester and eventually took voluntary redundancy from the Bank. Since then I've taken contract work and enjoyed the variety of different environments. I set up my own company, Big Blue Projects (www.bigblueprojects. com) to manage my speaking career, and any freelance marketing/ PR work and writing that I choose to do. I also kept in touch with Kim at YachtPals and I'm now a regular contributor to www. yachtpals.com! I even went back to La Gomera and Antigua to report on the Atlantic Ocean rowing race two years on!

I've taken the sailing a step further and completed my Coastal Skipper qualification – still feeling the need for a regular 'ocean fix' to keep me sane. Well, sane-ish! I enjoy helping people who are looking to take on the challenge of rowing an ocean, and I worked with the An-Tiki raft project in 2010. Led by 85-year old broadcaster and journalist Anthony Smith (no relation) and project managed by balloon pilot to the stars, Robin Batchelor, the An-Tiki crew of four successfully sailed a raft made of plastic pipes from La Gomera to the British Virgin Islands.

In 2011, I was selected for the GB Women's team at the World Dragon Boat Championships in Tampa, Florida. It's not something that I'd ever planned to go back to, but a great challenge to take on helming such an awesome team again.

As for the future... well, who knows! I still believe everything happens for a reason, so just have faith, believe in yourself and it all becomes clear in time!

And always remember, worse things happen at sea!

Appendix 1 – The supporters view

When we were in Antigua, my brother wanted to write a guest blog to describe how our challenge had been for him. It gave me a great insight into the emotions my family had experienced while I was out at sea, but also how proud they really were. We've expanded the blog a little, now time has passed...

This is the story from the other side. The story from the supporter's point of view - about two women rowing across the Atlantic and their welcome back to dry land in Antigua.

It's a very strange sensation when someone sits you down and tells you that they want to row across the Atlantic – I mean, how do you react to a statement like that? If I'm honest I can't remember much about what was said, just that it was a bit too much to take in all at once. All I could picture was Lin and Rachel bobbing along at sea in a rowing boat borrowed from the local park boating lake! But soon everything was explained and I could begin to understand what the months ahead might bring. I knew that for Rachel to tell me it was going to happen, she had thought it through properly and knew what she was doing, so I had blurted out my support within minutes!

The next few weeks were a flurry of excitement. Before I knew it I was taking bags full of collection tins, Breast Cancer Care badges, key rings, pens and notebooks into work and sending an email around the office asking for donations. My work colleagues were all extremely supportive and showed great interest in both the challenge and the charity. Every time there was a new magazine article published it did the tour of the office. Day by day I watched the fundraising total swell on the website through their generosity and that of my friends outside work. I think that's when the feeling of pride really set in – and my life was taken over by ocean rowing. It was all I could talk about and I must have bored people senseless!

Time really does fly when you are waiting for someone so close to you to do the unbelievable and December 2007 seemed to arrive within weeks of the initial announcement. The night before Mum, my partner Dave and I flew to the Canaries I didn't know how to feel. I only slept for a couple of hours as I couldn't settle due to a mixture of excitement, fear of the unknown and a sudden lack of understanding of how big the challenge actually was. The next time I would see Rachel would be on La Gomera, where she was already getting things ready for the start of the race with my 'adopted' sister Lin.

As soon as we reached the island we felt the sense of family between the ocean rowers. They are a strange crowd – so determined and focused, yet so welcoming and friendly – we were definitely made to feel part of the whole experience. There wasn't a lot we could do to help (apart from Mum trying to explain to a pharmacist that she wanted to buy a mini first aid kit by miming the different contents), so we took time to enjoy the island and photograph anything even vaguely related to ocean rowing. Seeing Barbara Ivy on the water for the first time during the 'parade' settled some of my nervousness – at least we could see for ourselves that she would float fully laden! It was great for me to spend so much time with Rachel before the race start day. I couldn't understand how she was so calm compared to me, but looking back, I think that is where her coaching background comes in – this was just the next stage of her journey, one she knew without doubt that she could complete. She'd waited a long time and worked so hard to be ready to start the race.

The morning of the race start soon arrived. Breakfast was a bit quieter than previous days, but seemed to liven up a bit when I produced the Christmas and Birthday presents that I had hidden under the table for both Rachel and Lin. Mum did the same but on a grander scale, so much so that Rachel asked where they were meant to store them all on the boat! I also presented them with Sebastian the ship's bear as a mascot for the journey. The next time I saw him was when he was all strapped in on the wall of the cabin, ready to go on his big adventure as the final preparations were completed.

The time had come. Family and friends were urged to go to the other side of the harbour so we could sit on the harbour wall to watch the boats make their wary journey to the start line. Each and every boat was cheered as they left the harbour. Seeing Barbara Ivy, Rachel and Lin row past was the real beginning of the emotional roller coaster. I have to admit the tears welled up even this early in proceedings, but that was nothing in comparison to the floods that couldn't be stopped at the sound of the starting horn.

Sebastian the Ship's Bear – all strapped in and ready to go!

The walk back to the square in San Sebastian was slow and numb. I don't think I will ever forget that strange mixture of feelings – pride, emptiness, happiness, sadness, fear, elation, closeness to others yet wanting to be alone, confusion, sickness and excitement all rolled into what felt like a large ball of emotion deep in my stomach. I don't think I had really considered it in the run up, but the realization that this wasn't going to be easy suddenly hit me, along with the fact that it really was possible for something to go wrong. It wasn't a nice feeling, but it was soon overtaken by the huge burst of pride that couldn't be held inside.

Back at home I settled into the routine of my new found sport of "dot watching". Each boat was tracked online by a different coloured dot on the map on the race website. This on its own often raised more questions than answers, especially when Barbara Ivy's position wasn't updated (when the tracker failed) or she seemed to be travelling in the wrong direction. The updates from the race organisers were relatively infrequent at times and this left us unsure as to whether everything was all right or not. But the excitement of occasional photos of Barbara Ivy and the girls that had been taken by the support yacht more than made up for this.

Before the girls had set off, Dave and I had pretty much decided that we wouldn't be able to afford to go to Antigua to see the girls arrive. But on the flight back from the Canaries

I changed my mind. Nothing would stop me from going. As I was in charge of updating the blog on Rachel and Lin's website I had to buy a laptop so I could carry on posting their updates wherever I was – each message bringing with it the usual mix of emotions that I was beginning to get used to. Being able to do the updates enabled me to feel I was contributing to, and part of the whole experience. This was the only contact I could get from Rachel and Lin due to the costs and power draining ability of the satellite phone. This made Rachel's birthday on Christmas Eve, Christmas Day and New Year a bit of an emotional period. Normally the first phone call between Rachel and I in the early hours of New Year's Day results in me reminding Rachel how old she will be next year. Childish I know, but New Year's Day 2008 meant I should have been able to tell her she would be 40 next year - I had been looking forward to it for years! Unfortunately though Rachel tried to call, she couldn't get through so we had to settle for a time later in the day and I know it was one thing that really upset her.

The strangest things give you comfort in situations like this. I found that the harder times for me were soothed by going outside on a clear night and looking at the stars. I knew that no matter where in the ocean Rachel and Lin were, they would at some point be looking up at the same stars as me. It seemed to bring me some sort of connection to them that I was missing when I couldn't talk to them.

I also found that sending them messages helped me, possibly as much as it helped the girls. Knowing that the messages that I sent would cheer them up, or give them a bit of a boost on the days they were missing home just made me feel like I was making a difference. Some of my messages were just for information or an update, others to celebrate a milestone in the experience, and others just for fun, like teasing them because I was sitting at home, all warm and dry, eating Cadbury's Crème Eggs. I won't mention the names I was called for that!

Like hundreds of people, we checked the website numerous times a day, until the time finally came for us to fly out to Antigua to welcome Rachel and Lin at the end of their tremendous journey across the Atlantic. The girls knew Mum was going to Antigua, along with Lin's Dad, John and son Liam. Our Aunt and Uncle were also there. However, unknown to Rachel and Lin, Dave and I also flew out to greet them. During their time at sea, Mum kept in constant contact with Rachel and Lin, so that we could ensure that we made it to Antigua in time for their arrival. The planning wasn't easy at all, but with great thanks to Lin's friend Jo, and Caroline at ABSAR, we were able to book a fantastic villa, very close to Nelsons Dockyard, where the girls were due to land.

As the girls didn't know that Dave and I would be waiting in Antigua, we had to keep up the pretence of being at home. This is where the laptop came into its own as I was able to sit outside the café in English Harbour, updating the blog and sending the girls a final message to say I would see them when they got home (and not to forget my bottle of rum!). I later found out just how well this all worked!

The day of their arrival was a flurry of activity. The two solo men's boats arrived during the day, one of which we were able to watch. But we started with a mad dash round one of the local supermarkets to make sure the villa was stocked with everything the girl's had been missing while they had been away. Cold bottled water and Diet Coke were top of the list

As the day went on we were given ever changing estimated arrival times for Rachel and Lin. The day just seemed to drag on and on and the waiting was unbearable. All I wanted now was to see the girls arrive safely.

With many thanks to Pete Collett's family (especially for the flares) Dave and I were encouraged to walk to the headland to see the girls make their final approach around Cape Shirley. This wasn't quite as easy as first thought because night had drawn in, so a quick sprint back to the villa for torches was called for. The track to the headland was steep and rocky, with uneven steps placed in 'strategic' positions, so it wasn't the best route for a pitch dark night.

Within minutes of arriving at the fort at the end of the headland, we could see a light shining in the distance. First thoughts were that it was a light on the rocks surrounding the narrow entry to the harbour. Then I realised that the light was slowly moving. Even better than this, it was being followed closely by another light! Still not being sure that it was Barbara Ivy, but with anticipation and excitement building, we held our breath until the faint glow of the orange ABSAR RIB could be seen.

Unlike when the previous boat arrived, the ABSAR RIB didn't light its bright orange light outside the harbour entrance, so we just couldn't quite be sure. But as the lights came closer, we could vaguely make out the pale blue outline of the deck and back cabin of Barbara Ivy. I couldn't take it in. Turning to Dave I whispered "I think it's them!" The tears started to flow again, making me laugh at the same time thinking how daft I would look if it wasn't them. After missing the girls for 76 days the sight of them getting closer didn't seem real until there was a sudden flash of light from the dots of reflective tape the girls had put on Barbara Ivy in La Gomera. They'd made it!

The ABSAR boat seemed to light its bright orange light as soon as we spotted the reflective tape on Barbara Ivy. Pete's parents had told us not to let the flares off until they were level with us, otherwise the girls wouldn't be able to see them and the impact would be lost. The waiting at this stage was painful and seemed to last forever.

The yachts and boats closest to the mouth of the harbour started sounding their horns and shouting to the girls and almost every word could be heard up on the Fort. As Barbara Ivy approached the headland, the excitement was building until I couldn't wait any more and set off the first of my flares. The effect was magical. Apart from signalling to those waiting on the dockside, the entire harbour and sky lit up with a red and white glow as we stood there waving them in – knowing full well that Rachel and Lin didn't have a clue that it was Dave and I that were welcoming them back to land. Emotional isn't the word for it. All we can say is if you ever get the chance to do the same don't let it pass you by.

The sounds from the boats in the harbour got louder and louder and were soon joined by the cheers and horns from the waterside restaurant. The noise level was increasing dramatically as we made our way rapidly back to the quay. I can't express in words how difficult it is to run over uneven and rocky ground, through the trees, with stone steps here and there and eyes full of tears while trying to see what is happening on the water. The view was amazing and Barbara Ivy was racing in (although the girls denied it, she seemed to be moving quicker than we expected!). By the time we arrived back at the quay, the girls were a matter of feet away and the whole dockside was a mass of cheering people, flares and horns. The only word I can use is 'magical'.

Perfect steering allowed the girls to pull Barbara Ivy right up to the quayside. I'm sure this must have been extremely difficult with the ever-increasing decibels from land. The first thing the girls needed to do was remove their harnesses and change into the Breast Cancer Care t-shirts they had saved for their arrival. One of the main rules on Barbara Ivy was that both Rachel and Lin would wear their harnesses at all times when they were on deck. This was a rule that we later found out had potentially saved their lives during the capsize.

This was swiftly followed by the girls lighting their own flares - made even more spectacular, knowing that the girls have completed this journey in order to raise money and the profile of Breast Cancer Care. The flares, although red, gave off a strong pink glow to the night sky – the pink signifying support for those dealing with and surviving breast cancer all over the world. As many of the supporters will know, the girls used Champagne to mark special occasions and milestones along their journey and they had saved the most special bottle for their final destination.

This bottle was given to them by Ainsley Harriott when they appeared on Ready Steady Cook. (Ainsley - If you happen to read this, please could they come back to tell you about their journey. They need feeding up now!) They opened the Champagne and promptly soaked each other and the waiting supporters at the same time as Amanda from the race organisers was returning the favour.

It was about this time that Lin spotted me and said to Rachel 'You'll never believe who I've just seen.... It's your brother!!' She couldn't believe it! The girls had always said that they wanted to leave the boat together. So holding hands, they were pulled onto dry land, as one, by Amanda and Lin's Dad, John. I don't think any of us could get close enough to them as they were swallowed up by the crowd. It isn't possible to put into words the feeling of immense pride and joy to see the girls finally arrive on dry land. But before long Lin told us about the capsize and explained why they hadn't mentioned it while they were at sea. There wasn't a dry eye on the quayside as they relived the ordeal, but not telling us was definitely the right thing for them to do.

Cameras were flashing all around and I don't know how the girls handled the number of questions they were being asked. The whole sensation of dry land and noise and family and friends that they had been missing must have totally overwhelmed them. Although a little wobbly and unsure of their steps, the girls managed to walk to the banners and balloons kindly provided by Breast Cancer Care (Thank you Christina) for more photos and of course, pink Champagne. More importantly than the Champagne, the fresh water and Diet Coke was waiting for them to enjoy. Mum will be able to testify the problems we had keeping it cold and ready for them. It isn't at all easy in the heat in Antigua!

We arranged for a taxi to take the girls and the essential

equipment from the boat to the villa. Lin was struggling with her foot and ankle injuries and both were still a bit unsteady. Although there was plenty of food in the villa, all they wanted was a cup of tea and some hot buttered toast! Both of these were a luxury the girls had missed and talked about on-board. But I don't think either of the girls expected to feel so desperate as to stick their heads in the fridge to enjoy the feeling of the icy coldness, or to be so amazed at seeing a toilet flush for the first time in over 2 months!

We heard a few more stories from the sea, before the girls attempted their first night sleeping on dry land. The stories have not ended since and we all hope they never will. We have all been with them through the highs and the lows, but only by hearing the reality can we ever begin to understand what they have been through. The remainder of our time in Antigua was full of emotion. From the girls writing postcards to the supporters to say they had arrived, and my friends David and Keith making an extremely generous donation even though neither had met the girls, to the newly recognised luxury of spending precious time with people you feel so close to and proud of.

A proud, happy brother and his little big sister!

It wasn't an easy journey for the girls but I know they would like to pass on their thanks to all their supporters across the world, who helped them through the hard times, and made the good times even more memorable. Please don't forget what these two remarkable women have done through their amazing journey and the bravery and commitment that both have shown. I will always look back and consider myself extremely lucky to have been part of such an amazing challenge. I wouldn't have missed it for the world!

With thanks to all supporters of the team - Gordon (Rachel's brother).

Appendix 2 - A day onboard

A day onboard Barbara Ivy – we stayed on GMT for the whole of our crossing which did mean dawn and dusk were later than you might expect. Most of the jobs were shared between us. We also took time off for meals and ate together which meant that our day 'rolled' and helped make sure we didn't always get the same hours of rowing and resting – so we both got to see different times of the day.

05.50　Wake up and stretch aching bits. Snack on half a Snickers bar and decide what to wear for rowing session (well what do you expect from a girls team?).

06.00　Rowing session in the dark.

08.00　Finish rowing session as it starts to get lighter. Then back inside the cabin to sleep. Wake at 09.50 to stretch and finish Snickers bar. Plot position on chart and log daily mileage.

10.00　Swap over for next rowing session. Lin checks the battery charge and goes inside to sleep.

12.00　Swap over for rowing session. By now it is too hot to sleep inside the cabin. Use the time for personal hygiene (a baby wipe bath) and running the water maker. Snack on fruitcake.

14.00　Check the battery charge and cook lunch (i.e. boil the water!). Stop rowing and eat together - an 800-calorie meal each. Discuss progress and strategy for next 24 hours.

14.30　Start rowing session. Still too hot to sleep in the cabin so we'd discuss what to include in the blog. Carry out repairs and adjustments for any equipment in need. Record the text messages received. Maybe call another rowing team for news.

16.30　Lin takes over rowing. Write diary and blog for the day and send it to the web site along with any photos. Favourite snack food included pretzels, mini cheddars, chocolate – while treats were a rare tin of fruit or Bailey's mini to wash down a meal!

18.30   Swap over for my next rowing session. Lin updates the text message log.

20.30   Finish rowing session and check battery charge. Lin heats water for dinner and we eat another 800-calorie meal together as the sun sets. Log our position.

21.00   First night time rowing session for Lin. Now cool enough to sleep in the cabin again. Use some rest time to phone home for a chat.

23.00   Wake up 10 minutes before session and stretch. Choose snack, clothes and music to listen to. Rowing in the dark again, gazing at the stars!

01.00   Swap over with Lin and head back inside the cabin to sleep. Snack on peanuts, raisins and chocolate chips.

03.00   Wake up 10 minutes before session and stretch. Choose snack, clothes and music to listen to. Be thankful that another night was nearly over.

05.00   Swap over with Lin and back inside the cabin to sleep. Too tired to snack!

07.00   Wake up 10 minutes before session and stretch aching bits. Snack on half a Snickers bar and plot position on chart. Start all over again!

Appendix 3 - How we coped

There were numerous times during this challenge when we were both tested beyond out limits, yet we stuck it out and made it all the way across. Often it would have been far easier to give up, but that wasn't part of our plan and we knew we would regret it if we did. So here's an insight into a few of the techniques and tools we used to keep us going in the really tough times.

1.   Set a goal and picture it in your mind. Then turn it into an experience and develop the picture in your mind, add colour and sound, imagine how it will look and feel when you achieve it. What will it sound like? Will you be able to touch it, taste it or smell it?

I had a vivid picture of the finish embedded in my mind. For some reason I had always imagined a night finish, with my family smiling in the bright lights. I dreamed about the first taste of cold fresh water, or beer! And could see the pride on my Mum's face as she gave me that first, longed for hug. I ran this through my mind over and over again, like a movie, especially in that incredibly hard final week. And the reality was better than I ever imagined!

2.   Control the controllables! One we brought from our dragon boating days. During your preparations, consider all eventualities and leave no stone unturned. Take control of every little detail that you are able to and reduce the risk of something that is genuinely out of your control from becoming a disaster. Even if you can't control what happens, you can control how you react to it. You have the power to choose whether you find solutions or find excuses.

Later on, we used a similar technique to help feel stronger and more powerful. In any situation you can stop and take control of more than you think, so when we were shaken up after the capsize, we planned and talked about our response and chose our favourite food for dinner. We played Chris Moyles on the iPod to make us laugh again. Neptune might have scared us, but he couldn't affect some things… we could take control right back.

In a tough situation, think about someone you admire or who inspires you; your hero. **How do you think they would they react in your situation?** What advice would they give you?

I used this technique during the long days of battling North. I thought about Debra and what she might say if I could talk to her, or how Dee Caffari might handle the soul destroying-ness of it all right then.

One piece of advice we received was **'when eating big elephants, take small bites'**. Basically, when you're faced with a seemingly impossible task, too big to take in, break it down into smaller, achievable goals.

During our preparations we set goals like 'getting to the start line', but there were a million and one smaller things we needed to do (goals to achieve) in order to make that happen. So we listed them and ticked them off one by one. It might sound obvious, but it's vital that you know when you've achieved a goal, so make a point of acknowledging it and maybe give yourself a reward. Likewise we set distance goals while we were rowing – 500 miles, a quarter, 1,000 miles, halfway, then the countdown to Antigua. Normally our little rewards were the tiny bottles of Champagne or Baileys!

3. What's stopping you? As Henry Ford said, 'If you think you can or you think you can't; you're probably right'. If you continually think 'I can't' or 'I could never do that', the chances are that you never will. So ask yourself 'What's stopping me from doing xxx?' You might be surprised with the answer and once you know what the obstacle is, you can set about solving it.

Lin and I faced exactly this with regard to the row. But when we asked ourselves what was stopping us, it was actually the money. We truly believed we could take on the challenge, even if that belief was based on 'if Debra rowed the ocean on her own, then surely between the two of us we stand a fighting chance!' So once we'd narrowed the main barrier down to money, we just needed to find a way to raise a small fortune. Simple!

4.   How would you recount the situation to someone else?
On some of the tough days I'd imagine telling the story once I
got home. To family, friends or an audience during a speech. By
thinking about how to describe what I was feeling and experiencing
to someone else, it took me out of the 'moment' and made it seem
almost like it was happening to someone else.

So for instance, lets take the intense, eyeball popping pain of
rowing against the wind and waves and being pushed south so
many times. Instead of simply sobbing with frustration and pain
(though that did happen!), I would imagine talking about it 'It
was an incredibly difficult part of the row, although it was hot and
sunny, we were battling on every stroke and could really feel the
effects. Rowing into the waves meant they would break over the
bow and soak you from behind, just adding insult to injury.' I'm
not sure how or why it worked, but it did!

5.   A good old laugh. I'm normally a pretty positive person
and naturally look for the plus points in most things. Of course I
do get down sometimes, but generally bounce back pretty quickly.
I know that laughter is a great solution to so many things, boosts
your mood and bonds a team together. We laughed a lot out at sea,
at the silly things that happened and funny things we'd noticed.
Sometimes though, we did find there wasn't much to laugh about
at all.

At those times we consciously did things to lift our mood and
make us laugh. We'd reminisce about funny (normally naughty!)
things we'd done and scrapes we'd gotten out of. We'd listen to
comedy on the iPod – Dara O'Brien and Chris Moyles were great
favourites. And even in the most desperate times, we found we
could simply laugh at the ridiculousness of our situation. I mean,
two naked-ish blondes and a pink boat, capsized 300 miles from
land and mostly worried about dinner floating away on the next
wave!

6.   Music for any occasion. Even back in our dragon boat
racing days, we both used music to help us along. Music can be
a powerful tool for inspiration, a calming influence, focusing,

feeling strong… there's a song for every moment. I used an iPod when I was rowing and we also had a portable battery powered speaker system that was waterproof enough to use on deck.

Many songs took on new meaning out at sea and even now, there are certain tracks that move me to tears as I picture the night sky, sprinkled with stars as I rowed alone in the darkness (such as Take That, Rule the World from the Stardust soundtrack). My choice of music eventually led Lin to the conclusion that I'm actually a closet Rock Chick. When we ran out of swear words to use, we were inspired by some rap songs! And although neither of us can sing a note, we made the most of the space and belted out our favourite lyrics over and over again.

Some of my favourites albums were Seal (Best 1991-2004), Tears for Fears (Tears Roll Down), Guns & Roses (Greatest Hits), Dandy Warhols (Thirteen Tales from Urban Bohemia), Gorillaz (Demon Days), Supertramp (Retrospectacle) and anything by Joss Stone or Jack Johnson. Pretty eclectic huh?! Barbara Ivy seemed particularly fond of a bit of Jack as she bobbed across the waves too!

7.   Count your blessings. Let's not pull any punches, sometimes I hated the ocean and being out there. But from the back of my mind I could easily recall the real reason we were putting ourselves thorough this. The money we raised for Breast Cancer Care would go towards helping countless people cope with their diagnosis, treatment and hopefully recovery. We still had choices; we chose to do the row and we could always choose to give up, though that wasn't really likely! But we often reminded ourselves that those with cancer don't have the same choice; they have to cope with what's thrown at them.

On New Year's Day, one of the worst days when we were both in tears, we got a text message from a lady in the UK. It said that what we were doing was giving her mother the strength to carry on with her cancer treatment. That one message gave us strength. It was incredibly humbling and put things in perspective for us. We soon started to look at things more positively. We don't know who that lady was and she'll probably never realise how important her words were to us – but she gave us a boost when we most needed it.

210

8.   Nothing replaces good preparation. Planning, being organised and leaving no stone unturned is simply the only way to be in the run up to any challenge. The ocean doesn't have favourites, it treats everyone the same, pushing you beyond your limits, and from this comes the respect of being a small speck on a large expanse of planet.

Out on the ocean our mental preparation really paid off and we firmly believe it was an important part of our success. We also found we were able to become far more inventive, resourceful and resilient than we ever imagined. At the end of the day though, you still have to know that during your adventure what will happen, will happen… but it will pass.

Appendix 4
Equipment onboard Barbara Ivy

Boat
Boat
Paintwork & logo stickers
Trailer
Storage (boat before and after row, trailer during row)
Lighting board & cable
Trailer lock
Straps
Boat Equipment
Plastic Hatches
Guard wire & mountings
Rudder fittings
Fixings - screws/bolts/nuts
Anti foul
Internal hatches
Watertight deck hatches
Filler
Harness eyes
Cabin locks
Ensign, pole, socket
Water ballast
Bearers - timber
Mooring lines
Internal lights
Jackstays
Cleats - foredeck & transom
Cabin padding/mattress
4 x handrails outside hatch
Skin fittings
Scupper gates
Towing eye
Fenders
Tripping line cleats for sea anchor
Rowing Equipment

Oars
Seat Padding
Set of rails & spares
3 seats (one complete spare)
Stretcher & straps
Pins & spares
Sheepskin
Gates & spares
Spare wheels
Associated Costs
Shipping
Race Entry Fees
Flights & accommodation
Satellite phone bills
Insurance
On Board
Notebook computer (Panasonic Toughbook)
Video recorder
Sea anchor & tripping line
Anchor and chain
Gimballed cooker & spares
2 x sleeping bags
Rope/warps & bridles
Dry bags
Kettle, pans, cutlery
Drogues
2 x waterproof torches
Elasticated netting & bungy cord
Waterproof storage bags & tubs
Solar battery charger
Cabin storage separation
Mugs, bowls, cutlery
Water bottles & cages
Tarpaulin
Pillows
Box for 'todays things'
Flasks
Internal/external clock
Windex
Alarm clocks
Food & water
Desalination machine

Food
Watermaker equipment & spares
Clothing & Hygiene
Foul weather gear x 2
Breathable t-shirts & shorts
Tilly hats
Travel towels
Sores/rubs kit
Domestic cleaning products
Toilet/bedpan
Loo roll
Electrical
Solar Panels
Flexi solar panels x 2
Iridium satellite phone & aerial (and spare phone in grab bag)
2 x marine batteries
Battery splitter
Battery monitor
Switch panel
Regulator with shunt
Short wave radio
Fixed compass
Wind speed gauge
3 x handheld GPS (one in grab bag)
2 x fixed GPS
Hand held compass x 2 (reverse card)
Navigation light
Hand held volt metre
Ships log, plotters & dividers
External aerial
Blocking diodes
Safety
Ocean life raft (ISAF and Solas B)
EPIRB 406
PLB (in grab bag)
First aid kit – specific for an ocean crossing
Sea-me radar enhancer
2 x lifejackets
Sunglasses
Flares RORC
Collision flares

Bilge pump & pipe work
Tool kit
Tracking beacon
2x three point elasticated lifelines
2 x harnesses
Seasickness tablets
2 fire extinguishers & fire blanket
Sun cream
Life jacket spares
Fog horn
Hull scraper
Fishing line
Hand bailer
Extras
Towing vehicle – SsangYong Rexton
Car & boat insurance
AIS system & antenna
Cabin bilge
Music – iPods and speakers etc
Charts
Video camera
Waterproof cameras

Appendix 5
Atlantic Rowing Challenge numbers

4 years	Length of the project from start to finish
3 years 1 month	Time it took from agreeing to do it to reaching the start line
3,500	Baby wipes onboard!
2,935	Miles across the Atlantic Ocean
33,680	Miles travelled round the UK for the project
£70,000	Cost of taking part in the race
£65,000	Raised for Breast Cancer Care
£550,000	Of PR coverage generated (AVE)
5,000	Calories allowed each per day – though we ate far less
90 days	Of food rations onboard
3 days	To be able to stand and walk normally again in Antigua
10 days	For our legs to stop hurting in Antigua
76 days, 11 hours and 12 minutes	To row across the Atlantic Ocean!

Appendix 6 - Glossary

ABSAR – Antigua & Barbuda Search and Rescue. An organisation manned by volunteers and sustained by donations, ABSAR provides medical and other support for those who need it, both at sea and on land. Operates in a similar way to the RNLI in Britain.
AIS – Automatic Identification System. A relatively recent addition to the marine world. Similar to a radar screen, it can identify registered vessels to each other and provide valuable information on route, speed, size, etc.
Antifoul – painted cover on the hull of a boat to discourage growth of marine life.
Baby wipes – often our only means of keeping clean. Became like currency onboard!
Bailers – small scoops used to clear water from the foot well. We also used a larger volume hand pump. We had an electric bilge pump too but could only use this on days when we had sufficient power.
Bow – the front (or in our case when rowing 'it's behind you!').
Broadside – sideways to the boat. As in, 'the wave hit us broadside!'
Bulkhead – vertical partition designed to contain water to an area inside a boat.
Cabin – front cabin used for storage. The rear cabin (aka 'the bedroom') was where we slept and was normally the only near-dry haven onboard.
Capsize – a 360-degree roll over by the boat.
Chandlery – a specialist shop for marine and boating equipment.
Cooker – a camping trangia and normal camping gas canister. Mounted on a wooden surround to help keep the wind out. We used wind proof matches to light it.
Desalinator – or watermaker. A machine that uses a process called reverse osmosis to extract salt from sea water, making it drinkable. The resulting drink tasted brackish and disgusting, with the texture of milk, and we hated it. But advancing technology means that new machines produce water that tastes amazing!
Dreadlocks – developed nicely after 6 weeks without washing our hair!

Drogue – small parachute shaped device, deployed from the bow or stern to reduce speed and/or increase stability.

EPIRB – Emergency Position Indicating Radio Beacon. When activated it will notify rescue services in minutes and provide valuable information about your position and the vessel it's registered to. A last resort!

Expedition food – freeze dried, high calorie meals that needed to be rehydrated with hot (or cold) water before eating. They all tasted pretty yukky after 76 days at sea – a bit like baby food mush for grown ups!

Foot well – the only area of the deck that wasn't self-bailing and therefore frequently full of ocean. Where we kept our toilet bucket!

Gate – a tough metal and plastic contraption to hold and secure the oars. They take a battering on the ocean but we only broke one during our crossing.

GPS – Global Positioning System. Uses a network of satellites to pinpoint position and allows you to plan and track a route. We could have used a sextant, but they're not so effective or easy to use onboard such a tiny boat. So we took 5 separate GPS units… back up for our back up!

Gunwale – the sides of the boat above the deck.

Jackstays – a line running the length of the deck used to clip our lifelines onto. Worked very effectively in keeping us attached to the boat when we capsized!

Knock down – when the boat tips over 90 degrees or more but rights itself without inverting.

Nautical mile – units of distance used in marine navigation. Equal to one degree of latitude or 1.852 metres (1.15 landlubber miles).

Nav light – Navigation light. A 360 degree white light used at night onboard small vessels.

Port – the left hand side of the boat when facing the bow. Aka 'chunder' on the first night!

RIB – Rigid Inflatable Boat. A very robust, relatively small powerboat with a solid hull and inflatable 'tubes'.

RNLI – Royal National Lifeboat Insitution. The UK's maritime lifesaving organisation. Manned by volunteers and sustained by donations from the public.

Rowing machine – we used WaterRower machines to train on land. They use water in a big bulb to create resistance as you row and allow rowers to exercise without a boat in sight.

Rudder – removable carbon fibre fin bolted to the stern to steer the boat. Controlled by lines running down the sides of the boat and attached to the left rowing (steering) shoe.

Satellite phone – Reminiscent of the 1980s mobile phones, the brick as we fondly called it was our lifeline to friends and family. But with calls costing in the region of £1 per minute, use was rationed!

Scuppers – holes in the side of the boat, level with the deck. Allow water to drain (self-bail) from the deck.

Sebastian – our Ship's Bear, given to us by Gordon the day we set off and named after San Sebastian, our departure port in La Gomera.

Sikkaflex – incredibly sticky stuff to cement and seal things onboard boats. Sticks to absolutely everything (including me!) and is unmovable once stuck. 'Sikkaflex it' became Ned and my war cry while we were working on the boat – a solution to any problem!

Sea anchor – aka para anchor. Large parachute-like device deployed from the bow (or stern). Slows progress significantly, can prevent being blown backwards and stabilises the boat in rough conditions.

Starboard – the right hand side of the boat when facing the bow. Aka 'Huey' on the first night!

Stern – the back of the boat. Aka 'the other end'.

Sudacrem – normally used for babies bottoms, but worked fairly well on rowers sore butts too!

Support yachts – Sara of Douglas and Kilcullen with their amazing crews who sailed up and down the fleet sharing encouragement and tales of pizza!

Tracking beacon – automatically sends position information every hour... when it works!

VHF Radio – marine radio requiring an operators' license. Your primary means of communication with vessels within your in line of sight (approx 4-5 miles).

Weebles – egg shaped children's toy from the 1970s. Weebles wobbled but they didn't fall down. Provided hours of fun!

Lightning Source UK Ltd.
Milton Keynes UK
UKOW04f0741020614

232691UK00001B/10/P